An Introduction to Classics

A short guide to the world of ancient Greece and Rome

Graham John Wheeler

Felicla Books

London

Published in the United Kingdom in 2015 by Felicla Books

Copyright © Graham John Wheeler, 2015

ISBN: 978-0-9931141-1-3

ALSO BY THE SAME AUTHOR

Classical Therapy: How Greek philosophy can change your life

Contents

1. Who were the Greeks and the Romans? 6

2. Homer..38

3. Ancient Languages and Getting Lost in Translation 62

4. Gender, Sexuality and Satire by a Conservative....................94

5. Philosophy and Religion in a World Full of Gods.................120

6. Tragedy and Some Tragedians...152

7. Oratory and the Orator 180

8. History Writing and Two Roman Historians 206

9. The Countryside in Reality and Imagination 238

1. Who were the Greeks and the Romans?

This is a book about two vanished civilisations which died out centuries ago. Why have I written it, and why should you spend time reading it? Why bother with the Greeks and the Romans?

The first reason is that the Greeks and the Romans were our cultural and intellectual ancestors. We are their heirs and their legacy still lives today. If there is such a thing as Western civilisation, and if we are part of it, then the Greeks and the Romans are our forebears, the people who lie at the roots of our own society. Studying them has the same interest, and builds the same sense of identity, as an individual researching her family tree. Classical studies teaches us where we come from, and in doing so helps us to understand how we got here and who we are. On this view, classics is a kind of civilisation-wide version of *Who Do You Think You Are?* The Greeks and the Romans are family.

And there are a lot of family resemblances, sometimes in unlikely places. A large part of the contents of the average art gallery cannot be understood without a knowledge of ancient art and mythology. The most basic political concepts cannot be discussed without drawing on Graeco-Roman vocabulary – *democracy, aristocracy, dictator, monarch, emperor, republic, oligarchy, tyranny* – in addition to *politics, civic, government* and many others. If you go to a church or a graduation ceremony, you can still hear Latin being spoken amidst an architecture of classical pillars and architraves. If you take the Eurostar to Paris, you can still hear the French speaking what the humourist Henry Beard called "badly mispronounced lower-class provincial Latin". The philosopher A.N.Whitehead said that Western philosophy is a series of footnotes to Plato. If you drive up the A6 or the A10, you will be following the routes of roads originally built by the Romans.

By any standards, classical civilisation is deeply embedded in British and European culture, and by extension in the cultures of the United States and the Commonwealth countries. It is a recurrent fact of history that we have ended up turning, or returning, to the ancient world when searching for intellectual and artistic resources to use in renewing our own societies. This was the case in the Renaissance (to take the best-known example), and again in the Enlightenment of the 18th century. We have continually reinvented our classical heritage, constantly using and reusing it to meet our changing needs. Ancient Graeco-Roman thought and literature have served as an inexhaustible quarry of ideas for successive generations to rediscover, borrow and argue about. It is a bit like the way that, after the fall of the Roman Empire, the mediaeval Greeks and Italians physically quarried construction materials from the remains of the classical buildings around them in order to use them in new structures. The difference is that the ancient world's legacy of ideas never runs out.

Another good physical metaphor for this process is the Pantheon in Rome. This large, imposing circular building near the centre of the city was originally built in 27 BC as a temple for the Roman gods (and was subsequently rebuilt again a couple of times for the same purpose). With the coming of Christianity, it was rededicated as a Catholic church, *Sancta Maria ad Martyres*. Finally, with the advent of the modern Italian state in the 19th century, it became something of a temple of Italian nationalism, housing the tombs of members of the royal family. Uniformed monarchists continue to stand vigil there. The building also served as a model for other "Pantheons" in countries ranging from France and Portugal to Bulgaria and Georgia, and these have served variously as places of religious worship and temples to secular national heroes. So it is that the classical inheritance is constantly renewed and reinvented – always changing, always the same. The Greeks and the Romans aren't "vanished civilisations" at all – they remain part of our cultural DNA.

Yet there has also been a tendency among some scholars to emphasise the deep differences between the Greeks, the Romans and us – ancient culture is "desperately foreign", to use a phrase popularised by the great ancient historian Sir Moses Finley. This tendency is not just a recent trend confined to iconoclastic academics. The great Victorian headmaster Thomas Arnold said much the same thing in reference to the teaching of classics in 1840:

> ....[T]he very difficulty which is often found in realizing the things of which we read, the difficulty of representing to ourselves times so remote, and so unlike in many respects to our own, shows how much the mind requires such a discipline, and how naturally it rests contented with the scenes immediately around it. (*Sermons Chiefly on the Interpretation of Scripture* (London: Longmans, Green & Co, 1878), 180)

It is not difficult to illustrate the foreignness of Graeco-Roman society. "Democracy" didn't mean then what it means now – it meant not elections for a parliament but *every* citizen voting on *every* major decision. In this context, a "citizen" was a free adult male – the status and treatment of women, and indeed of slaves, would strike the modern observer as alien if not barbaric. When *we* discuss the issue of women wearing veils in public, for example, the context is whether we should ban it, not whether we should *require* it. The experience of walking through ancient Rome would have been more akin to walking through Rangoon or Nairobi than strolling past the Armani and Versace boutiques on the Via del Corso today. Modern science students do not expect to pick up a textbook on atomic physics and find that it is – like Lucretius' ancient Roman work on the subject – written entirely in poetry. I could go on. From this perspective, studying classical culture is still useful, but in the same way – and only in the same way – as studying, say, Chinese or Mayan culture.

At the end of the day, the question of whether the Greeks and the Romans were like us or were essentially alien is unanswerable. The Cambridge classicist Robin Osborne has called it an "unreal dichotomy". Worse, it misses the point. It is as futile as discussing whether the *Odyssey* is "like" or "unlike" James Joyce's *Ulysses*. It is the very *mixture* of the comfortably familiar and the utterly different which makes classical studies so fascinating. Classics is a gateway into two enormous world civilisations, with all the variety and contradictions that all great cultures have within them. The Greeks and the Romans were like us, and yet they weren't. A lot of the time, they weren't even like themselves. The Greeks were rational and superstitious; democratic and despotic; artistic and warlike. The Romans were conservative and licentious; legalistic and brutal; cosmopolitan and parochial. There is something in there for everyone.

In this little book, I want to act as a tour guide around a few of the more accessible parts of the vast continent of classical antiquity. I will start, in this chapter, with a brief introduction to the Greeks and the Romans – who they were and what they said about themselves. The succeeding chapters focus more specifically on particular topics and texts, starting with the epic poems of Homer, which were in many ways the foundation stone of Graeco-Roman culture. I will assume no prior knowledge of the ancient world beyond the sort of general knowledge that might come up in a crossword or a pub quiz. All I hope is that I leave you wanting more. Classical civilisation is an enormous field of study: I can make the introductions, and then the rest is up to you.

*

Let's start with the Greeks.

To begin with, there *were* no "Greeks". Our earliest texts, the epic poems of Homer (c.600s BC), have little evidence of a common Greek identity. Homer's Greek and non-Greek (Trojan) characters share the same culture, religion, political institutions and even language. The Greek characters are referred to collectively using several different terms, but the standard later term *"Hellénes"* is barely even mentioned.

The idea of Greekness seems to have taken shape only at a later stage. There is a famous passage in the great *History* of Herodotus (c.484 – 425 BC) in which the Athenians appeal to the Spartans in the name of "our common Greekness [*Hellénikon*], with the same blood and language, and our common shrines of the gods and sacrifices, and our common customs" (8.144). This has often been taken as the quintessential definition of Greek identity. It is too brief and incidental for that, but it remains as good a summary as any of what it meant to be Greek. Note that it includes both shared ethnicity and shared cultural features. The cultural features are in turn a mixture of the physical (e.g. temples) and the intangible (e.g. the Greek language). Being Greek meant sharing a package of common characteristics which the Greeks themselves didn't take much trouble to define too narrowly.

12

By Herodotus' time, the Greeks also knew who they *weren't*. They weren't barbarians from the East – the peoples of the Persian Empire, the superpower of the day which had twice tried and failed to turn Greece into a subject province. Their language was incomprehensible - just a lot of *bar bar bar*, hence the "barbarian" label (*barbaros* in Greek). The Asian barbarians were stereotyped in Greek literature as weak, cruel, luxurious and servile – unlike the manly, freedom-loving Greeks. These prejudices were only reinforced by the fact that many of the slaves which the Greeks encountered in their own city-states happened to be from the East. The great philosopher Aristotle had this to say:

> The peoples in cold regions and in Europe are full of spirit, but are deficient in intelligence and artistry; so they have continued to live in relative freedom, but they are politically disorganised and have not managed to establish rule over their neighbours. The peoples of Asia are intelligent and naturally given to artistry, but they are fainthearted; so they have continued to live like slaves under authoritarian rule. The Greek race, however, shares in both sets of qualities, just as it is geographically in the middle. It is spirited and intelligent, so it has

continued to live in freedom and has been governed the best. It could rule over all peoples, if it managed to create a single state. (*Politics*, 1327b)

The tables were later turned on the Greeks by the Romans, who portrayed them in a vaguely similar manner to how they had portrayed their eastern neighbours. The Romans referred to them in this connection as *Graeculi* – "little Greeks" or "Greeklings". Modern scholars have also challenged the Greeks' self-image by emphasising how much they owed culturally to those supposedly barbaric Asian societies.

So the Greeks did come to see themselves as being, in some sense, a "nation" – although we must be careful with this terminology. Many historians would be reluctant to speak of "nations" before the rise of modern nationalism and the nation-state. At any event, like everyone else, the Greeks thought that their "nation" was the best one in the world and that by being born into it they had won first prize in the lottery of life. The philosophers Thales and Socrates were said to have given thanks to the goddess Fortune that they had been born humans rather than animals, men rather than women, and Greeks rather than barbarians (Diogenes Laertius, 1.3).

As the quote from Aristotle above suggests, however, "national" unity was never a strong feature of Greek civilisation. J.C.Stobart, the author of a onetime bestseller entitled *The Glory that was Greece* made the point that Greek society was fiercely localistic and parochial:

....Nature has split [Greece] up into numberless small plains and valleys divided from one another by sea and mountain. Such a country, as we see in Wales, Switzerland and Scotland, encourages a polity of clans and cantons, each jealous of its neighbour over the hill, and each cherishing a fierce local patriotism. (J.C.Stobart, *The Glory that was Greece* (London: Sidgwick & Jackson, 1911), 29)

Stobart's analogies are slightly surprising – Athenian high culture was a long way from *People of the Valley* – but he had a point. Classical Greek civilisation was born and flourished in the small city-state or *polis*, a form of political (literally, *poli*-tical) organisation which was quite different from anything that we are used to today. As an example of this, it has been pointed out that the Elgin Marbles from the Parthenon in Athens have consistently been seen in modern times as a symbol of Greek nationality, whereas in ancient times they were a much more specific symbol of the *polis* of Athens.

During the golden age of Greek civilisation, Greece was a patchwork of broadly similar but endemically squabbling *poleis*. This arrangement worked well enough for several centuries, until Alexander the Great (356 – 323 BC) and his family came down from Macedonia and swallowed them up in an empire. One research project, the Copenhagen Polis Centre, counted 1,035 *poleis* throughout the Greek world. They weren't just in modern-day Greece, either – the Greeks founded settlements throughout the Mediterranean and beyond, from Russia in the east to Spain in the west.

At this point, it might be useful if I set out a crude summary of Greek history, in the form of a list of the periods which scholars have traditionally divided it into. This can act as a general map of the territory that we are going to be travelling through; feel free to refer back to it as necessary.

- **1600 to 1100 BC – Mycenaean period.** The earliest period of Greek civilisation, based around a series of great palaces ruled by a warrior aristocracy. The term "Mycenaean" comes from the city of Mycenae, the site of one of the palaces.

- **1100 to 800 BC – Dark age.** Mycenaean civilisation collapses and Greece goes through a cultural recession which lasts for several centuries.

- **800 to 500 BC – Archaic period**. The *polis* emerges as a social unit. The epics of Homer are composed, along with other early works of Greek literature. Greek settlements – "colonies" – spread throughout the Mediterranean and beyond.

- **500 to 300 BC – Classical period**. The high point of Greek art, culture and civilisation. Also a time of endemic warfare between the Greek *poleis* and against foreign foes. The period is brought to an end with the coming of Alexander the Great and his family, who incorporate Greece into a huge multinational empire.

- **300 to 146 BC – Hellenistic period**. The Greek world is ruled by Alexander's kingly successors. Greek scholarship and philosophy continue to flourish in Athens and the Egyptian city of Alexandria (named after Alexander). The period ends when the Romans arrive and absorb Greece into their own empire.

This kind of list gives a slightly misleading impression of Greek history, because it makes it look much neater and more uniform than it actually was. There are also various rather tedious debates about precisely where to draw the lines between the different periods. Nevertheless, the list gives us somewhere to start.

Going back to those squabbling *poleis*, it is not difficult to find examples of Greek parochialism and localism in the ancient sources. One of the most famous is the "Funeral Speech" of the great Athenian general and statesman Pericles (c.495 – 429 BC). This is imaginatively recorded by the historian Thucydides (c.460 – c.400 BC), who also happened to be an Athenian general. The speech may not accurately represent what Pericles actually said – ancient historians were allowed to be creative when putting speeches into the mouths of their characters. It does, however, provide a useful summary of how the classical Athenians chose to see themselves. Note in particular how it asserts the superiority of Athens over her rival Sparta, which she was then fighting in a deadly conflict known as the Peloponnesian War. The speech was delivered in honour of Athenian troops who had been killed in the conflict.

> Our form of government does not enter into rivalry with the institutions of others. We do not copy our

neighbours, but are an example to them. It is true that we are called a democracy, for the administration is in the hands of the many and not of the few....

Our city is thrown open to the world, and we never expel a foreigner.... And in the matter of education, whereas the Spartans from early youth are always undergoing laborious exercises which are to make them brave, we live at ease, and yet are equally ready to face the perils which they face....

For we are lovers of the beautiful, yet simple in our tastes, and we cultivate the mind without loss of manliness....

To sum up: I say that Athens is the school of Greece, and that the individual Athenian in his own person seems to have the power of adapting himself to the most varied forms of action with the utmost versatility and grace. (*History*, 2.35-46; trans. Benjamin Jowett (adapted))

So there you have it. The Athenians were not only tough but also cultured and democratic – unlike those dour authoritarian Spartans, who lived in a highly conservative and militaristic society. Predictably enough, this flattering view of Athenian civilisation was not universally shared amongst other Greeks.

Thucydides himself says that most Greeks supported the Spartans and saw the Athenians as oppressive imperialists (the Athenians were both democrats and empire-builders – any modern parallels?). Thucydides also knew that Athens eventually lost the Peloponnesian War, and it is clear from other parts of his history that he was not a friend of democracy. The Funeral Speech is ostensibly a celebration of a vibrant, living civic culture, delivered in memory of men who had died fighting to defend it. But there are hints even within the speech itself that Thucydides was actually writing the epitaph of a society which he knew was fragile and was already living on borrowed time. What was he thinking, for instance, when he immediately followed the speech with an account of a particularly virulent plague which fell upon Athens? It would seem that all that "cultivating the mind without loss of manliness" didn't do the Athenians much good in the end.

Those dour authoritarian Spartans left behind less literature than the Athenians, perhaps predictably. But one quotation attributed to King Ariston of Sparta can serve as a riposte to Pericles' fine rhetoric:

When one of the Athenians read a memorial oration in praise of those who fell at the hands of the Spartans, he said, "What kind of men, then, do you think ours must be who vanquished these?"

This comes from a collection of quotations known as the *Spartan Sayings*, which are attributed to various figures from Spartan history. The sayings are typically short, blunt and militaristic – literally *spartan* and literally *laconic*, Laconia being a term for the region of southern Greece where Sparta was located. Here are a few more of them:

He said that the Spartans did not ask "how many are the enemy," but "where are they?"

Androcleidas the Spartan, who had a crippled leg, enrolled himself among the fighting-men. And when some persons were insistent that he be not accepted because he was crippled, he said, "But I do not have to run away, but to stay where I am when I fight the opposing foe."

When Dionysius, the despot of Sicily, sent costly raiment to Archidamus' daughters, he would not accept it, saying, "I am afraid that, if the girls should put it on, they would appear ugly to me."

As he was listening to a musician, he said, "He seems to do his silly task fairly well."

When someone said, "Why have you not killed off the people of Argos who wage war against you so often?" he said, "Oh, we would not kill them off, for we want to have some trainers for our young men." (Trans. F.C.Babbitt)

These sayings are entertaining, and they may reveal something about the mentality of the Spartans. But they also reveal something else. The *Spartan Sayings* were not published by Spartans. They were compiled, if not invented, by non-Spartans who were interested in or impressed by the Spartans' reputation for courage and manliness. The collection represents, at least in part, an exercise in myth-making by people who had their own agenda. So, indeed, does the history of Thucydides. And so, to some extent or other, does all writing about the past, including our own writings about the Greeks and the Romans. This is something that we need to constantly bear in mind.

Going back to Athens, the view of Athenian civilisation which Thucydides puts into Pericles' mouth was not necessarily shared universally amongst the Athenians themselves. For example, the bawdy and surreal comic plays of Aristophanes (c.450 – c.388 BC) don't lend much weight to the idea that classical Athenian culture represented "the utmost versatility and grace", although they do remain funny even today. On a political level, the democracy thing stuck in the throats of some conservative writers. One of the many surviving texts from 5th century Athens is a diatribe by an entertainingly bigoted aristocrat known as the Old Oligarch. He had no truck with any modern Periclean one-man-one-vote nonsense. He thought that democracy just served the interests of the lower classes, who were characterised by "ignorance and indiscipline and worthlessness". Plenty of other wealthy men across Greece would have agreed with him.

*

As for the Romans, the great poet Virgil (70 – 19 BC) tried to write their mission statement for them. In his towering epic, the *Aeneid*, Virgil depicts the Roman founding father Aeneas journeying to the underworld. There, his dad Anchises shows him various figures from future Roman history before telling him what sort of people his descendants will be:

> Others will be more skillful at beating breathing forms of bronze –
> yes, I believe it – and drawing living faces from marble;
> they will plead cases better, and will better trace the heavens'
> paths with a measure and predict when the stars will rise.
> But you, Roman, take heed – you must rule the nations with
>   empire.
> These will be your arts – to bring peace with civilisation,
> to spare the defeated and to bring down the proud in war.
> (*Aeneid*, 6.847-853)

This is literature, but it is also propaganda for imperial Rome. A few lines before, Virgil had incorporated a personal guest appearance by his friend the Emperor Augustus Caesar ("the son of a god, he will found a golden age"). So we need not take Virgil entirely at face value. There is also an obvious irony in the fact that a claim that the Romans were practical military men rather than artistic nancy boys appears in the middle of one of the greatest works of literary art ever produced by the human mind.

The contrast being drawn by Virgil in the passage above is between the Romans and the Greeks. As we have noted, the

Romans engaged in a certain amount of stereotyping of the Greeks, portraying them as over-educated and effeminate. They couldn't help but admire their cultural achievements, however. A similar sentiment to Virgil's is famously found in a poem by his contemporary Horace (65 – 8 BC):

> Captured Greece captured her rough conqueror and brought
> the arts to bumpkin Latium; so that the coarse
> Saturnian metre faded away, and elegance
> banished rough gut-rot; but still, after long years,
> traces of the farm remained and remain today.
> (*Letters*, 2.1.156-160)

The "Saturnian metre" was an archaic Roman form of poetic metre. The Romans took most of their poetic metres from the Greeks, as well as most of their literary genres – epic, tragedy, comedy, elegy and so on. Satire alone was a Roman invention. We will be meeting one prominent Roman satirist in Chapter 4.

Another, less triumphalist view of the Romans' place in the world was put forward by the historian Livy (c.59 BC – 17 AD). Livy was the author of a monumental multi-volume history of Rome, *From the Foundation of the City*, a significant portion of which still survives. We will be looking more closely at this work in Chapter 8. For the time being, we can confine our attention to Livy's preface:

> I ask each reader to focus his mind carefully on these things: how we lived, how we conducted ourselves, who were the men and what were the skills, at home and at war, by which our empire was established and expanded. Then let him trace with his mind how, as discipline gradually weakened, our morals first began to decline, then fell further and further, and finally began to dive headlong, until he reaches the present time, in which we can tolerate neither our vices nor the cures for them....
>
> But, unless I am deceived by love for the subject which I have taken up, no state has ever been greater or more pious or richer in good examples, nor is there any nation where greed and luxury have been so late in arriving, nor where there has been such honour paid for so long to poverty and frugality, so that the less wealth we had, the less desire we had for it. In recent times, riches have brought greed, and freely available pleasures have brought a desire for destroying ourselves and everything else though luxury and hedonism.

Presumably not everyone would have agreed with Livy's take on things, but he was a very popular writer and it is a fair bet that what he says in this passage would have reflected the outlook of many upper- and middle-class Romans of conventional views.

Livy was writing at a time when Rome was enjoying an unparalleled period of strength, prosperity and peace, so his complaints about civic decline ring a little hollow. They become more comprehensible, however, when we consider that the notion of national decadence was a stock theme of Roman writers – and there was some degree of truth to it. For Rome, imperial expansion and increasing wealth had carried a cost in the form of increased political corruption and violence. The old republican constitution of the state had been deliberately set up to be both competitive and restrictive. It was difficult to get to the top of the political tree, and once you had got there it was difficult to stay there. Even the heads of state, the two Consuls, served only for a one-year term, and the fact that there were two of them placed an obvious check on each Consul's authority. In the Roman Republic, politics was a game that no-one could really win.

The result was an overwhelming temptation to cheat. In the course of the 1st century BC, Rome saw the rise of a succession of military strongmen – Marius, Sulla, Pompey, Julius Caesar – and several rounds of civil war. Eventually, Augustus (reigned 27

BC – 14 AD) came along and ended the game by setting up an imperial monarchy. It couldn't be *called* a monarchy, though – the Romans had had a bad experience of being ruled by kings in the distant past, and the word for "king", *rex*, was taboo – a bit like the word "tyrant" in English. The title usually translated as "emperor" was *princeps*, "chief".

The new imperial system could be described as a vaguely constitutional monarchy. The old republican Senate and magistrates continued to exist and continued to hold limited and varying degrees of power. It was still well worth being a Consul, for instance. Only much later, with the coming of the Emperor Diocletian (reigned 284 – 305 AD) did the system turn into a full-blown absolute monarchy, in response to a severe military and political crisis which nearly finished off the Roman state altogether. But that is another story.

Now seems like a good time for another list, this time to illustrate the different periods of Roman history:

- **753 to 509 BC – The regal period.** Rome is founded by the legendary hero Romulus and is ruled by a succession of kings. The year 753 BC is the traditional date for the foundation of the city: it is basically a guess, and seems to be about a century or so too early.

- **509 to 27 BC – The Republic**. Under the rule of a republican constitution, Rome develops from a small Italian city-state to a world-ranking empire. It defeats its main rival, the African state of Carthage, and extends its rule from Spain to Syria and from Belgium to Egypt. In the last 50-100 years of its life, the Republic slowly falls apart and is replaced by.....

- **27 BC to 284 AD – The Principate**. Under the rule of a vaguely constitutional monarchy, the Roman Empire reaches its zenith of power and cultural greatness.

- **284 to 476 AD – The Dominate**. The Emperor becomes an absolute monarch and the Empire fractures into eastern and western halves. Christianity becomes the official state religion. The western half of the Empire is overrun by barbarians, while the eastern half evolves into the Byzantine Empire.

A disproportionate number of first-rank Latin writers date from the period of the collapse of the Republic and the reign of Augustus. Several of them were personally connected with Augustus and his right-hand man Maecenas, who has gone down in history as a patron of the arts. These writers included Livy, Horace and Virgil. Livy was on good terms with the imperial family, even though Augustus apparently suspected him of Republican sympathies. He is a conservative writer in several senses of the term, which perhaps explains the sentiments in the passage quoted above. However, the theme of moral decline was not confined to establishment conservatives. It was famously taken up again by the later imperial historian Tacitus (56 – c.120 AD), an altogether more spiky and cynical character who liked to affect an anti-establishment pose.

Tacitus is an interesting guy. To a large extent, the stereotyped image of imperial Rome as a place filled with orgies, violence and mad emperors is derived from him – the result of people taking his lurid and carefully crafted "histories" at face value. In particular, Tacitus was a major source for Robert Graves' historical novels and the 1976 BBC TV series *I, Claudius* that was based on them. Three generations of viewers have now been introduced to Augustus, Caligula and the rest through the imaginative filters of Tacitus, Graves and the television scriptwriter Jack Pulman. This is a good example of how the classical world can be creatively borrowed into modern culture. At what point in the process we start to lose contact with "real" history is wide open to debate. You may not think it even matters very much, any more than it matters whether Shakespeare got his facts exactly right about Henry V or Richard III.

Anyway, back to Tacitus and his preoccupation with moral decline. A good example of his views can be found in his monograph *Germania*. This is a famous work of ethnography on the ancient Germanic tribes which has captivated generations of readers up to and including the Nazis. At this point, Tacitus is talking about the women of Germany:

> This is how they live, their modesty protected, uncorrupted by alluring public shows or sensual banquets. Clandestine letters are unknown to men and women alike. Adultery is very rare in such a large nation; punishment is immediate and lies with the husband. With her hair cut off, stripped naked, and watched by her relatives, the husband expels the wife from the house and drives her with blows all through the village. No quarter is given to easy virtue: neither beauty nor age nor wealth will find the girl a husband. No-one there laughs at vice. They do not call it "modern" to corrupt and be corrupted. (*Germania*, 19)

We will have more to say about ancient attitudes to sex and marriage in Chapter 4. Suffice it to say here that Tacitus' words illustrate not only his distaste for modern-day Roman society but also his liking for the idea of the noble savage. The counterparts of decadent Romans were uncorrupted barbarians. The noble savage theme appears elsewhere in Tacitus' works too – most famously in *Agricola*, a biography of his father-in-law Gnaeus Julius Agricola. This little work contains extended passages dealing with ancient Britain, where Agricola had served as a general. Tacitus was not really on the Britons' side politically, any more than he wanted the Germanic barbarians to overrun the Roman Empire. But he admired their wildness and freedom, and he seems to have felt that something was lost when they submitted to Roman rule and the trappings of Roman culture:

> So too our dress became prized and the toga worn often. Gradually, the Britons lapsed into the temptations of vice – colonnades and baths and sumptuous banquets. This in their naivety they called "civilisation", when it was part of their slavery. (*Agricola*, 21)

This is still history written by the victor: it is unlikely that Tacitus made any serious attempt to ask the Britons themselves for their side of the story. But it is nevertheless a different vision of Rome's mission and place in the world from those of Virgil, Horace and Livy. It may even seem oddly familiar. In more modern times, writers in Western imperial and post-imperial societies have fallen prey to the temptation to idealise colonised peoples in much the same way as Tacitus did, from native Americans to the tribal peoples of the Pacific.

It should come as no surprise that not all Roman writers were patriotic or moralistic. Still, nothing quite prepares the beginner for something like this:

> I'm going to rape your arses and rape your mouths,
> Aurelius, you poof, and Furius, you queer.

These lines are not taken from graffiti in a toilet in Pompeii – they are the beginning of a well-known poem by a highly erudite and polished man of letters called Catullus (c.84 – c.54 BC), who lived about a generation before Livy. Roman high culture is not all lofty declamation and strict moralism. Catullus is not everyone's cup of tea – some find him precious and too clever by half – but he is a paid-up member of the literary canon. Literature is not always a business for maiden aunts.

Catullus is remembered mainly for his poems about his love affair with "Lesbia" (Clodia Metelli, the sister of a controversial left-wing politician). Catullus was followed by a series of other love poets in the early years of Augustus' reign, notably

Propertius, Tibullus and Ovid. Their works are sometimes seen as being a challenge to the new imperial regime. Augustus was attempting to pursue socially conservative policies as a means of restoring stability to the war-torn Roman state. The typical love poet, by contrast, subverted orthodox Roman values by avoiding marriage and family life, portraying himself as subservient to a woman and rejecting actual military service in favour of the "soldiering of love" (*militia amoris*). There is a vague comparison to be made here with rock musicians in the age of Vietnam and Nixon.

The most gifted of the Augustan love poets, Ovid (43 BC – 17 AD), ended up being exiled by Augustus, and blamed it on his risqué poem *The Art of Love*, along with another unnamed "error". This claim may be disingenuous – some scholars think that the poem was merely a pretext and that Ovid's real mistake was to offend Augustus through his mysterious "error" (a scandal involving the imperial family? a political offence?). Whatever the truth may be, Ovid took the subversion a step further than everyone else. He not only mocked traditional Roman morality, he also mocked his fellow poets for taking themselves too seriously.

Ovid incorporates counter-cultural themes into his account of his own life, which he wrote in exile after he had fallen foul of

Augustus. A passage from his short autobiography will make a fitting end to this chapter. As a young aristocrat, his father had wanted him to pursue a respectable career in public life rather than become a poet. Ovid describes how he initially gave politics a try before giving up his senatorial rank – symbolised by a broad purple stripe on his toga – for a life away from the rat race. Read it as the ancient equivalent of an upper-middle-class teenager bent on making it as a bass player when his father wants him to become a lawyer.

> If it matters, I was heir to an ancient family line;
> I was not newly made a knight by fortune's gift....
> We began our schooling as young boys; our father took care
> to send us to men renowned for the City's arts.
> My brother leaned towards rhetoric from his greenest years,
> born for the harsh battles of the word-filled forum;
> but I loved the heavenly rites [of poetry] even as a boy,
> and the Muse secretly drew me to her work.
> My father often said, "Why bother with these useless pursuits?
> Homer himself left no wealth behind him."...
> I won the first civic honours of tender youth:
> I was once one of the Board of Three.
> The Senate awaited me; I narrowed the width of my stripe;
> that burden was too much for my strength.

My body could not bear the work, my mind was not fitted for it;
I sought refuge from pitiless ambition,
and the Aonian sisters [the Muses] called me to seek the safety
of leisure, which my tastes had always loved.
(*Tristia*, 4.10.7-40)

WHO WERE THE GREEKS AND THE ROMANS?

2. Homer

Western literature begins with Homer, the reputed author of two Greek epic poems known as the *Iliad* (the *Song of Troy*) and the *Odyssey* (the *Song of Odysseus*). There is a reason why Ovid's father used him as an example of supreme poetic genius. For the Greeks and the Romans, Homer was the ultimate cultural icon. He was their Bible and their Shakespeare. He was part of the air that they breathed. This was particularly so for the literate élite – the poet Horace recalled:

> I happened to be raised in Rome, where I was taught
> how much harm angry Achilles inflicted on the Greeks....
> (*Letters*, 2.2.41-42)

This is a reference to the main plot line of the *Iliad*, which is driven by the anger of Achilles, the great Greek warrior who was immortalised by Brad Pitt in the 2004 film *Troy*. It is probably only a slight exaggeration to say that everyone in the ancient world would have known who Achilles was and why he was angry. Knowledge of Homer wasn't confined to educated men of letters. He seems to have been widely known amongst ordinary people too, just as peasants in 17th century England might not have been able to read the King James Bible but would have known its stories and its turns of phrase.

Both the *Iliad* and the *Odyssey* deal with stories arising out of the Trojan War. This was a semi-legendary conflict between an alliance of Greeks and a city-state called Troy, which was located in the north-west of modern-day Turkey. The conflict was ignited when Paris, a prince of Troy, seduced and abducted Helen, the most beautiful woman in the world and the wife of King Menelaus of Sparta. Interestingly, it was Helen rather than Paris who tended to get the blame for this. Menelaus and his brother Agamemnon went to war in an attempt to recover the wayward woman, and their forces ended up besieging Troy for ten long years before they finally captured it through the stratagem of the Trojan horse.

The *Iliad* is based on an episode which was said to have taken place in the course of the war. Agamemnon, who is serving as the Greeks' commander-in-chief, makes the mistake of dishonouring Achilles, who duly goes on strike. The Greeks are left to fend for themselves without the help of their best fighter. One of the consequences of Achilles' extended sulk is that his beloved comrade Patroclus is killed by the Trojan prince Hector.

When Achilles finds out about this, he is enraged and returns to the battle. He ends up slaughtering Hector, and then further humiliates the dead man by dishonouring his corpse. In the final book of the epic, there is a superb episode in which Hector's father, King Priam, petitions Achilles to return the body to him; Achilles consents, and the *Iliad* ends with Hector's funeral.

The *Iliad* has always tended to be considered the greater of the two Homeric epics, but it is also the less accessible. Its extended battle scenes are not always appreciated by modern readers. With its military setting, relentless and graphic violence, largely male cast and consuming conflicts over honour and status, it has a distinct odour of the locker room. The epic may ring especially true to readers from a military background. Jonathan Shay, an American psychiatrist who worked with combat veterans, wrote a book called *Achilles in Vietnam*, in which he argued that Homer's characterisation was psychologically accurate. On a more mundane level, the great Oxford classicist Jasper Griffin wrote: "As a sixth-form boy I had no difficulty in recognizing the quarrel between Agamemnon and Achilles as a glorified version of the quarrels and contention in any gang of young men..." (*Homer on Life and Death* (Oxford: Clarendon Press, 1980), 52). This is not to detract from the complexity of the poem. It can certainly be argued that it questions and undermines the conventional macho values which it portrays. All the same, it's not everyone's cup of tea.

*

And so to the *Odyssey*. The *Odyssey* consists of over 12,000 lines of long, stately verse written in a stylised archaic dialect of Greek that was old even in Homer's time. The epic contains a single overarching story, told in a non-linear way, with several sub-plots. It is sometimes described as the first novel.

Like the ancient world generally, the world of the *Odyssey* is at once familiar and alien. The alien-ness comes not only from the fact that the poem's main character, Odysseus, is a legendary hero who mingles with gods and goddesses. It shows through in more mundane ways too. Odysseus inhabits a cultural world which has deep differences with modern Western society. Life in the ancient world was often tough, and the need for stability and security tended to take precedence over individual rights. The social ecology of archaic Greece was one of loyalty, authority and tradition rather than freedom, merit and social mobility. Someone who wants to understand the dynamics of Homeric society – and ancient Graeco-Roman society more generally – could do worse than watching *The Godfather*, or visiting certain parts of Bradford.

One important feature of archaic Greek society, which it shared with other pre-modern societies, is that individuals tended to occupy fixed social roles with fairly clear-cut duties and prerogatives attached to them. Aristotle, for example, tells us that people in different stations in life each have a different "function" (*ergon*) and "excellence" (*areté*). Peoples' roles were based on such things as sex (man, woman), occupation (farmer, merchant, artisan) and social status (aristocrat, citizen, immigrant, slave). For the most part, you did not choose your place in society: you took it from your father or husband, or from your surrounding circumstances. It was difficult – but not impossible – to move from one role to another. Meritocracy was considered less important than maintaining a stable, cohesive society in which people knew their place. You had limited opportunity to choose your job, to choose your spouse or to move into a higher social class. This is the backdrop against which the *Odyssey* must be understood.

The main plot of the epic is simple and well known. Odysseus, the sly and cunning King of Ithaca, was on the winning side in the Trojan War – in fact, he was the one who thought up the Trojan horse trick. After leaving Troy, he wanders the seas for ten years in an attempt to return home to Ithaca, having various adventures on the way. When he finally gets back home, he finds his palace occupied by a crowd of badly-behaved local princelings who are attempting to marry his wife Penelope and claim his throne. He disguises himself as a beggar, kills them, and restores things to their rightful order.

Put like this, the *Odyssey* sounds like a simple revenge drama, or even a morality tale, with some folk stories about journeys to foreign lands thrown in. But it is much more than that. Let's take the opening lines, which form one of the most famous openings in Western literature:

> Tell, Muse, of the many-turning man, who wandered far
> when he had sacked the sacred citadel of Troy:
> many were the men he met and the cities he saw,
> many the woes he suffered at sea in his heart,
> trying to save his life and bring back his comrades –
> but yet he did not save his comrades as he wished....
> (*Odyssey*, 1.1-6)

As this introduction indicates, the *Odyssey* is about estrangement and alienation – about wandering, homeland and return. The central theme of the epic is Odysseus' desire for a *"nostos"* (return) to his *"oikos"* (household), his *"philoi"* (loved ones) and his *"patris gaia"* (fatherland), from all of which he is currently separated. He desperately misses not only Ithaca as a place but also the social roles that belong to him there, as a king, husband, father and household-head. We are told that he would rather die than not return home. The goddess Calypso even offers him immortality if he will stay with her on her desert island, but he just isn't interested.

The basic message of the *Odyssey* is that you can't be a person without a context. This means finding both your correct geographical place and your correct social place. This is why, for example, characters in the epic repeatedly greet each other by asking where the other person comes from and who his parents are. For his part, Odysseus gives his address to people he meets as Ithaca, even though he hasn't been near the place for years. It is here that we find the true significance of Odysseus' wanderings. They are not merely colourful travellers' tales – although they are that as well. They present Odysseus in a series of unsuitable contexts as he attempts to return to his proper place. At one point, he himself sets out a kind of manifesto for the poem:

....Indeed, there is nothing
sweeter for me to look on than my homeland.

Calypso, the lovely goddess, kept me with her,

in her hollow caves, wanting me as her husband;

so too Circe kept me in her palace, the wily

woman of Aiaié, wanting me as her husband;

but they never persuaded the heart in my breast.

So, nothing is sweeter than one's native land and

parents, even if one dwells far off in a rich house

in a foreign land, away from one's parents. (9.27-36)

A contrast is repeatedly drawn between Odysseus' story and the story of his comrade-in-arms Agamemnon. As we have noted, Agamemnon was the brother of Menelaus and the commander of the Greek forces at Troy. He was married to Clytaemnestra, the sister of Helen. While Agamemnon was away fighting the Trojan War, Clytaemnestra was seduced by the villain Aegisthus; when Agamemnon came back home, Aegisthus killed him. The similarities and contrasts with the story of Odysseus don't need to be emphasised. The story of Agamemnon has a happy ending, of sorts, since Agamemnon's son Orestes turns up and kills both Aegisthus and his mother. Note that Homer attaches no moral guilt to this deed. Blood vengeance is an accepted institution, and we are supposed to think that Aegisthus and Clytaemnestra had it coming to them. This is not a world of police and law courts – it is a rural Mediterranean culture of family honour and revenge. We will see in Chapter 6 how the story of Agamemnon was handled in later Greek literature.

It isn't only Odysseus who needs to find his proper place. His son, Telemachus, who is waiting for him in Ithaca, is still trying to grow into his role as the young master of the house. The poem begins with a kind of boy-to-man novella (which has sometimes been called the *Telemachy*) in which Telemachus seeks to step into his father's shoes. He is initially introduced to us in Odysseus' palace as a powerless youth who is feeling bereft of his father and daydreaming about his return. Homer makes it clear that he looks and sounds like his dad, but he is not yet sure of his own identity. He is told by the goddess Athena that he needs to grow up quickly, and so he starts taking on Odysseus' role in the house and in the wider community of Ithaca. He ends up journeying around southern Greece looking for news of Odysseus, a journey which parallels both Odysseus' travels and his own metaphorical journey into manhood.

When Odysseus finally gets back to Ithaca in the second half of the epic, Telemachus continues the process of assuming the role of the young man of the household. Significantly, he turns out to be the only person other than Odysseus himself who is strong enough to string Odysseus' great bow. The final book of the epic, Book 24, depicts the reunion of three male generations of the royal family: Telemachus, Odysseus and Odysseus' elderly father Laertes. The parts of the epic dealing with Telemachus and his transition into manhood can still be read with some benefit by a male sixth-former today.

The *Odyssey* is notable for having prominent and well-drawn female characters – the goddess Athena, the goddess Calypso, a witch called Circe, a princess called Nausicaa, and of course Odysseus' beloved wife Penelope. At the start of the epic, Penelope is depicted as something of a weak, tearful woman. It is also made clear that, in normal Greek fashion, she is at the disposal of Telemachus, as the male head of the household, and that she would otherwise be under the tutelage of her father. But it quickly becomes apparent that she is not a woman to be underestimated. We hear the well-known story of how she staved off having to marry one of her suitors. She told them that she needed to finish weaving a shroud for her old father-in-law before she could get married, and she then made sure that she got up during the night and secretly unpicked each day's handiwork so that the task was never finished. All in all, Penelope is one of the most memorable characters in Homer. It is very significant that she is the only character in the *Odyssey* who ever succeeds in outsmarting Odysseus, the master trickster (I won't tell you how).

There isn't much doubt about Penelope's loyalty to Odysseus, even though she eventually gives in and agrees to marry one of the suitors just as Odysseus returns home. She *has* been bereft of her husband for twenty years, after all. Odysseus, being a man, is given freer rein to play away. He has sexual relationships with two female characters, Calypso and Circe, although Calypso complains that he keeps on talking about his damn wife all the time.

Homer's touching portrait of Odysseus and Penelope is one of the most charming features of the *Odyssey*. It is clearly important to Homer that the couple really love each other. His ideal for a married couple appears to be a state which he refers to as *homophrosyné*, "thinking the same". In other respects too, the epic shows a relatively nuanced view of relations between men and women. Take this passage, which describes Telemachus going to his bedroom accompanied by a slave-woman called Eurycleia:

> There he went, to his bed, with his mind full of thoughts;
> with him, carrying burning torches, went the wise
> Eurycleia, daughter of Ops, Peisenor's son;

Laertes had bought her long ago with his wealth,

for twenty cattle, when she was still a young girl;

he honoured her like his dear wife in the house,

but he never slept with her and angered his wife.

She brought burning torches with him; she loved him most

of the house-slaves; she had nursed him as a baby.

(1.427-435)

The reference to the three-way relationship between Eurycleia, Laertes and Laertes' wife is intriguing, but sadly Homer does not elaborate on it any further. It may seem surprising that Eurycleia, as a slave, has such intimate relationships with members of the royal family; but this, as we shall see, is part and parcel of Homer's ambivalent attitude towards social distinctions. No doubt there were real-life examples of such relationships too.

More generally, the *Odyssey* tells us a lot about what the ancient Greeks considered to be civilised values and behaviour. When Odysseus arrives in an unfamiliar place, Homer uses a stock phrase to describe what he is thinking about the inhabitants:

"Are they arrogant and wild and without justice,

or do they welcome strangers and think piously?"

In other words, to be civilised is to be welcoming to strangers and to be pious to the gods. As we might expect in a story dealing with travel, hospitality is a central concern of the epic. "Guest-friendship" or *xeinosyné* (*xenia* in later Greek) was a key Homeric social institution. It was a kind of sacred, institutionalised form of hospitality – particularly useful in an archaic society with no developed network of inns and guest-houses. It required a host to offer generous hospitality to a guest who arrived at his door, no questions asked, and it included the giving of *xeinia* or "guest-gifts". The guest was likewise supposed to behave graciously towards his host. Once a relationship of *xeinosyné* had been established, it could be passed down and inherited by the guest-friends' sons and grandsons. The legacy of these archaic ideas of hospitality has survived in Greek culture right down to the modern age.

In the *Odyssey*, civilised characters consistently observe the rules of guest-friendship, while uncivilised characters don't. Telemachus gives hospitality to Athena and receives hospitality from other characters while on his journeys. Odysseus is given particularly generous hospitality by the highly civilised King Alcinoos in a fantasy land called Scherié. The suitors who are occupying Odysseus' palace are perverting the institution by inviting themselves onto Odysseus' property and plundering his wealth. When Odysseus turns up in disguise as a beggar and becomes a candidate for *xeinosyné* in his own palace, they throw things at him. At the extreme, in the well known story of the cyclops, the cyclops sets about killing Odysseus' companions when they present themselves at his home, and tells Odysseus that his guest-gift will be the privilege of being eaten last.

As for piety and the gods, the basic framework is clear enough. The gods have power over human affairs, and human beings in their turn worship them and earn their favour through sacrifices – at least, they do so if they are dutiful like Odysseus. Odysseus' wanderings and homecoming are attributed to the will of the gods. We likewise hear of other heroes' wanderings on their way home from Troy, and these too are explained by reference to divine intervention. The gods sometimes mingle among humans in disguise, and they send dreams and portents. Odysseus' eventual triumph over the suitors is foretold by several omens.

All the same, it is not entirely clear who is ultimately in charge. "The gods", or even just "God", are spoken of as controlling events and as giving blessings and woes to mortals; yet individual gods have specific and sometimes opposing roles to play. Athena and Poseidon take opposite sides, working respectively for and against Odysseus. It is clear that Zeus is the supreme god, but there are limits to even Zeus's role: there is an interesting passage at the beginning of the epic where Zeus complains about humans blaming the gods for their misfortune when it's really their own fault (this comes off a bit like a politician complaining to his colleagues about the ingratitude of the voters). Elsewhere in the epic, we come across the concept of a "Fate" (*Aisa, Moira*) which seems to stand above the gods, and enigmatic characters called the "Spinners" who spin a thread for each human's life when he or she is born. There are definite tensions and inconsistencies in this picture, and Homer hasn't really attempted to resolve them.

The *Odyssey* is pervaded by references to the concepts of *kleos*, "fame" or "renown", and *timé*, "honour", as well as the opposite concept of *aiskhos*, "disgrace". Homeric society was highly competitive and was preoccupied with such ideas. The quest for *kleos* is a major theme of the *Iliad*. In that poem, Achilles famously said that he had chosen to have a short life winning fame (*kleos*) on the battlefield of Troy in preference to surviving and obtaining a safe journey home (*nostos*). Yet the *Odyssey* subverts the conventional value attached to *kleos*. When Odysseus visits Achilles in the underworld in the course of seeking his own *nostos* to Ithaca, it is made clear that his deceased comrade has made the wrong choice:

"No, do not speak well to me of death, glorious Odysseus.

I would prefer to live on earth as another man's serf,

the serf of a landless man, who has a scant livelihood,

than to rule over all of the decayed dead." (11.488-491)

The final book of the epic contains a prediction of the *Odyssey* itself, when the ghost of Agamemnon declares that Penelope will have *kleos* in song in future years on account of her faithfulness to her husband. In fact, Homer's celebration of Penelope extends some way beyond the stereotypical feminine virtue of fidelity – but then Book 24 is unsatisfactory in a number of ways, and seems to be a later addition to the text. At any rate, bardic epics like those of Homer served to preserve a great man's *kleos* in future generations, and in the *Iliad* Homer himself refers to heroic poetry as *"klea andrón"*, "the famous deeds of men". Interestingly, the notion of a man's heroic deeds winning *kleos* was very old even in Homer's time, to judge from the fact that the Homeric phrase *"kleos aphthiton"* ("undying fame") has a parallel in early Sanskrit poetry from India. The idea may go back to Indo-European society, which we will look at more closely in the next chapter.

The *Odyssey* and the stories told in it have resonated over the centuries with audiences in widely different places, times and cultures. This may be because it deals with widespread or universal human experiences – the pain of separation from one's home and family; the search to find one's place in the world; marital love; the feeling that life is governed by supernatural forces beyond one's control; the need for a boy to become a man; the idea that life itself is some kind of wandering or exile. The classical scholar Robert Fagles described the epic as "something like the autobiography of the race". It evidently has something important to say to us about the human condition – although, as with most great works of literature, what it says is ambivalent and open to some debate.

There is enough in the *Odyssey* to allow us read it as a deeply traditionalist, conservative text. It depicts an agrarian Mediterranean culture based on social hierarchy, the patriarchal family and ideas of personal honour. Its hero is a battle-hardened warlord. It is permeated with the ideas of needing to occupy one's proper place in society and of attachment to one's native land. It takes for granted the existence of monarchy, a class system and slavery.

Yet this broad-brush characterisation doesn't do justice to the complexity of the epic. Homer mostly upholds the traditional values of archaic Greek society, but he questions them as well. As we saw, he overtly undermines Achilles' heroic quest for *kleos*

54

as expressed in the *Iliad*. Likewise, Odysseus' longing and love for Penelope challenges and transcends the patriarchal frame of the plot, as does Penelope's own obvious cleverness. The slave-woman Eurycleia is loved and respected by Odysseus and his family in a way that sits uneasily with her status, and she refers to both Odysseus and Penelope as *"teknon emon"*, "my child". Social status is shown to be the product of chance: Odysseus' swineherd Eumaeus is of noble blood but finds himself working as a slave because he was captured by a gang of Phoenicians. Telemachus refers to him as *"atta"*, "daddy". While Odysseus is disguised as a beggar, he tells the suitors a plausible-sounding story to the effect that he is a nobleman down on his luck. Homer isn't exactly Che Guevara, but he does show an awareness that traditional norms and boundaries can be eroded by individual human relationships, and that social status is to a large extent a product of chance.

*

There was almost certainly no single individual called "Homer" (*Homéros* in Greek). The name was probably manufactured from that of the *Homéridai*, a class or clan of bards whom we know about from later sources. For the *Iliad* and the *Odyssey* are bardic texts, the work of traditional folk-singers rather than literate scholar-poets like Virgil, Horace and Ovid. They grew out of a long tradition of songs about gods and heroes which extends far back into the mists of time. A common form of entertainment in archaic Greece was for professional minstrels to sing to their aristocratic warrior patrons over dinner about the heroic deeds of their forefathers; the *Odyssey* itself contains scenes illustrating this practice. This appears to have been the context in which the Homeric epics took shape.

The epics bear clear traces of their origins in this oral poetic tradition, the best known being the use of repeated formulaic phrases ("wily Odysseus", "the wine-faced sea"), some of which take up whole lines ("And when early-born, rosy-fingered Dawn appeared"). These stock poetic formulae would have been invaluable to oral poets. Two American scholars, Milman Parry and Albert Lord, studied modern-day bardic singers in 1930s Yugoslavia in order to shed light on the process of composition and performance. They even discovered a kind of modern Homer, a Bosnian Serb singer called Avdo Mededović, who obligingly sang a couple of his own epics for them. On the other hand, some scholars have questioned how much such researches can really tell us about how things were done in early Greece. It has also been argued that Homer's use of the resources of the oral tradition was imaginative and innovative: when he uses formulaic phrases, he does so with some care and artfulness, not just because they are convenient tools for filling up the poetic metre.

There remain various unresolved issues surrounding the composition of the Homeric poems. These issues, which are known collectively as the "Homeric Question", have given scholars plenty to get their teeth into over the years. While the notion of a single towering genius called Homer owes more to myth than to history, many experts do believe that the *Iliad* and the *Odyssey* were fashioned out of the oral tradition by two specific individuals who lived in archaic Greece, one for each poem. Some have even argued that the *Odyssey* was composed by a woman. This theory was argued for at length by the Victorian novelist Samuel Butler. One of his proofs was that the first thing that Odysseus does after killing all the suitors is to *clean up the mess.*

In recent years, close study of the contents of the poems, together with external evidence, has suggested that they can be dated approximately to the 600s BC (previously, they tended to be dated slightly earlier, to the 700s). They are therefore several centuries older than the heyday of classical Greek civilisation in the 400s and 300s, when men like Herodotus, Thucydides and the great tragic playwrights were active (see the list of periods in

Chapter 1). The *Odyssey* would have been composed later than the *Iliad*, in part because it seems to presume that its audience already knows the other epic (the dig at Achilles and his silly ideas about *kleos* is one example of this). This theory doesn't mean that we have to adopt a romantic view of two lonely geniuses creating stunning world-class masterpieces out of nothing. It is clear that they would have been standing on the shoulders of the centuries-old bardic tradition. It is also accepted that some parts of the epics are likely to be later interpolations: Book 10 of the *Iliad*, for example, has been regarded with suspicion since ancient times, and we have already noted that Book 24 of the *Odyssey* doesn't smell quite right.

Other scholars dispute this reconstruction of events. They argue that the epics originated in the mists of time, but that they did not reach a fixed and unified form until quite a late stage. This may perhaps have been in the mid-500s BC, when the Athenian dictator Pisistratus had them edited for public performance – or it may not have been until the 200s and 100s, when academic editions of the epics were produced by scholars in Alexandria in Egypt. Theories of this sort are generally traced back to a German scholar called F.A.Wolf, who published a book on the subject in 1795, but they are older. Wolf and his successors, the "Analysts", thought that the two epics had been stitched together or worked up from older, shorter poems, and they duly sought to pick the epics apart into their alleged constituent pieces. This approach is now outmoded. These days, scholars of the "neo-Analyst" school are more likely to argue that the epics came into being not when discrete older songs were stitched together but rather when previously fluid texts came to be crystallised into a definitive form over a period of centuries. There is no room in this theory for two individual poets who put the texts into broadly final form in the 600s. The neo-Analyst view is not without its problems. The internal clues in the texts do consistently seem to point to a date of composition in or around the 600s: there is a lack of telltale anachronisms from later times to indicate that they were still evolving after this period. The language of the epics likewise seems to have resisted being "modernised" in later times.

At the other end of the spectrum, some have looked back into the depths of time for the origins of the Homeric poems. If the key event which overshadows both epics is the Trojan War, could it possibly be that their ultimate origins lie in a real-life war by Greek forces against a city called Troy? Was Troy in fact a real place? Was the Trojan War a real event? If so, were Odysseus, Achilles and the rest real people?

A key figure here was a German businessman called Heinrich Schliemann, who went digging for the remains of Troy in the 1870s. He knew where to look because Homer gives us various topographical clues about the location of the city, notably the fact that it was close to Mount Ida (modern Kaz Dağı) in north-western Turkey. Schliemann espoused a very optimistic view of what archaeology could achieve. "I have looked on the face of Agamemnon", he is supposed to have declared after finding a golden mask depicting some long-forgotten minor chieftain. Even today, Schliemann is a highly controversial character, and a lot of people would be happy to write him off as an incompetent fraud. But he did have the distinction of excavating, somewhat clumsily, a genuine ancient city which was located in the right place to be Troy. Among the remains, historians have identified a layer of destruction in the late 12th century BC, and some have suggested that the circumstances of this destruction formed the real-life model of the Trojan War. Outside the field of archaeology, references have been found in texts from other ancient civilisations to a place in the right area called *Taruisa* (in Hittite) or *Tw-r-s* (in Egyptian). The Hittite sources also refer to a city-state in the region called *Wilusa*, ruled by *Alaksandu*; these names resemble an early Greek term for

Troy, *Wilios*, and the name *Alexandros*, which Homer applies to the Trojan prince Paris.

These connections are interesting, but they must be treated with caution. Most scholars today accept that Troy was a real place, that Schliemann, for all his faults, managed to find it, and that wars were really fought there. What is much less certain is that Greek bards composing in the 600s BC would have had access to more than a faint ghost of a memory of events that had taken place half a millennium earlier. Bear in mind that any such memory would have been entirely dependent on the vagaries of oral tradition: the Greeks went through a cultural recession, in which they appear to have lost the art of writing, for several centuries between the heyday of "Taruisa" and "Wilusa" and the earliest plausible date for the composition of the Homeric epics (this is the so-called "Dark Age" referred to in the list of historical periods in the last chapter). There can be little question that Odysseus and the other Homeric heroes are figures of legend – although this has not stopped them from being real enough for generations of listeners and readers.

3. Ancient Languages and Getting Lost in Translation

For upper- and middle-class English people, classical studies would traditionally have begun with Latin lessons at school. This shared experience, frequently unpleasant as it was, has often been lampooned in English popular culture. Think of Mr Quelch, the classics master from Frank Richards' *Billy Bunter* books, Nigel Molesworth, the prep school Latinist memorably drawn by Ronald Searle, and John Cleese's grammatically fastidious centurion in *The Life of Brian*. The thousands of schoolchildren who continue to learn gerundives and the ablative absolute are the heirs of a very long tradition of Latin-learning. In fact, they have it pretty easy – in Shakespeare's time, it was common for European schoolboys to be required to speak *only* Latin, even when talking amongst themselves at break times.

For Latin was not just a language – on a par with, say, Spanish or Russian – it was the universal language of high culture and civilisation. A knowledge of Latin both marked a person as educated and gave him (or sometimes her) a key to the treasure house of the Western cultural tradition. The status occupied by Latin among the learned classes of Europe was captured almost poetically by the ultra-conservative philosopher Joseph de Maistre:

There is nothing equal in dignity to the Latin tongue.... Born to command, this language still commands in the books of those who spoke it....

It is the language of civilization.... Cast a glance at a map of the world, trace thereon the line where this universal language is no longer heard: that line is the boundary of European civilization and fraternity.... The Latin language is the mark of Europe. Medals, coins, trophies, tombs, primitive annals, laws, canons – all monuments speak Latin....

After having been the instrument of civilization, there was wanting to the Latin tongue only one species of glory, and that it acquired by becoming, in due time, the language of science. Men of creative genius adopted it as the medium for communicating to the world their great thoughts. Copernicus, Kepler, Descartes, Newton, and a hundred others of high note, although not equally renowned, wrote in Latin. An innumerable multitude of historians, theologians, writers on law, medicine, antiquities, &c. inundated Europe with Latin works of every description. Charming poets, and literary men of the first order, restored to the language of Rome its ancient forms, and carried it to a degree of perfection which ceases not to astonish all who compare modern writers to their early models.

Yet by Maistre's day Latin was already in decline as the common language of European civilisation. Europe's post-Roman "Latin millennium" ran from approximately 800 AD – which we may take as the point at which spoken Latin had evolved into the Romance languages – to 1800. The passage above is taken from Maistre's masterpiece *On the Pope*, which was published in 1819. Maistre was fighting a rearguard action. Yet the decline of Latin was a long, slow process, and even today it has not yet run its course.

Interestingly, the cultural dominance of Latin was not dependent on Roman political power. It may come as something of a surprise to discover that only a tiny minority of surviving Latin texts were composed while the Roman Empire was still a going concern, and most of those are late works by Christian writers. The big names from the classical period like Virgil and

Livy are only a drop in the ocean. This point has been made forcefully by the German scholar Juergen Leonhardt in his interesting book *Latin: Story of a World Language*. Leonhardt reports that the number of Latin epics written in mediaeval and even modern times is more than one hundred times greater than the number of Latin epics which, like Virgil's *Aeneid*, survive from the ancient world. Likewise, we only have 40 or so Latin plays from antiquity, whereas the number of plays staged in Latin between the 1400s and the 1700s is between 5,000 and 10,000. These are astonishing figures, and it is worth pausing for a moment to let them sink in.

Not only was Latin used long after people stopped needing to obey Roman proconsuls and trade with Roman merchants – it was used far beyond the boundaries of the old Empire, by peoples who had never fallen under its rule. The implications of this are often overlooked. Latin was used for centuries after the fall of Rome, by people who had never been Roman subjects, not because there was any ongoing political or economic pressure to do so but *because it was there*. People needed a common language for practical reasons, and Latin was a convenient candidate for the role. Indeed, it was the only serious candidate for the role. The language accordingly took on a life of its own. In a similar way, the educated *lingua franca* of the Roman Empire itself had been Greek, long after the Greek states had lost what political power they possessed. (The Romans barely noticed that any other languages *existed* – they could use the phrase *utraque lingua*, "both languages", without any further explanation being needed.) It will be interesting to see if the entrenched status of English as a world language survives the inevitable decline of Anglo-American geopolitical power in the same way. Will it just be easier and cheaper for everyone to continue treating English as the common standard instead of switching to Mandarin?

The last echoes of Latin are only now dying away. Latin was the official language of Hungary until the 1840s, and the constitution of one European state, San Marino, continues to be mostly written in the language. The EU occasionally uses Latin terminology. When "international" languages became fashionable in the late 19th century, Latin was seriously put forward for the role, alongside Esperanto, Volapük and other less worthy candidates. Some of English law is still written in Latin – notably Magna Carta, three clauses of which remain in force to this day. Latin words are still sometimes heard in the courts, although this sort of thing has fallen out of favour since a series of modernising reforms in 1999. British sovereignty over Gibraltar continues to rest on a document written partially in Latin, the 1713 Treaty of Utrecht. Every British coin declares that

Elizabeth II is *"D[ei] G[ratia] Reg[ina] Fid[ei] Def[ensor]"* – "By the Grace of God, Queen, Defender of the Faith". Until as recently as 2011, the international scientific convention was that newly discovered plants had to be described in Latin. A Finnish radio station, Nuntii Latini, broadcasts weekly news in the language.

The historic cultural dominance of Latin contrasts sharply with the fate of Greek after classical times. Greek has always been a language made up of different dialects – unlike Latin, which was relatively homogeneous until it broke up into Italian, Spanish and so on in the Middle Ages. In ancient times, texts in Greek were composed in a number of distinct dialects. These worked partly on a regional basis: for example, the "Attic" dialect spoken in Athens was different from the "Doric" dialect spoken in Sparta. They also differed according to literary genre: for example, pastoral poetry was conventionally composed in the Doric dialect even by writers who were not native Doric speakers. Modern translators have sometimes attempted to capture these differences through such desperate expedients as translating parts of texts written in Doric dialect into Scottish English.

The dominant Greek dialect came to be a dialect known as *Koiné*, "Common Language", which was similar to the Attic dialect of Athens. The ancient Greek language was preserved down the centuries in the form of Koiné through its use in the Bible and the rites of the Greek Orthodox Church. It never had the same influence as Latin, however – it was not a universal language of politics, science and literature. For example, when the Orthodox Church spread from Greece to new regions like Russia, the liturgy was translated into local languages. Matters were not helped when the Greeks ended up falling under the domination of the Muslim Turks (a development neatly symbolised by the conversion of the Parthenon into a mosque). For centuries, Greek as a living language was little more than the dialect of an ethnic and religious minority within the Ottoman Empire. In the West, ancient Greek was rediscovered by scholars during the Renaissance, but it never came close to challenging the place of Latin as an intellectual and political medium.

Greek was only rehabilitated as a modern national language in the 19th century, with the rise of nationalism and the establishment of an independent Greek state in 1832. There followed a controversy over which dialect of Greek should become the new national language – the common tongue spoken by ordinary Greeks, known as *Dimotiki*, or a scholarly form closer to ancient Greek, known as *Katharevousa*. In broad terms, Dimotiki ended up winning, although it took a long time to do so – Katharevousa only lost its official status as recently as 1978, following the fall of the last military dictatorship, and even then it lingered on to varying degrees in conservative institutions like the army, the Orthodox Church and the law courts. Standard modern Greek is essentially a somewhat elevated form of Dimotiki; attempting to speak pure Katharevousa is in most settings an invitation to be mocked as a pompous bore. Nevertheless, even the standard form of modern Greek is an unusually archaic language – considerably closer to ancient Greek than modern English is to, say, mediaeval Anglo-Saxon. A foreign speaker of the ancient language can make himself understood to some extent in modern Greece, although he should be prepared to be greeted with some amusement.

*

For those people who were spared the experience of learning Latin and Greek at school – which means the vast majority of people in the Western world today – the ancient world is something that is known only through translation. This may seem at first sight to be a relatively minor problem. Language barriers are real enough, but they can be surmounted – can't they? Well, yes and no. Translation can be a tough proposition. It is not just a matter of technical linguistic skill: it's also a matter of bridging the gap between different cultures and different styles of thought. For a classical scholar to translate Homer into English is not just a more difficult task than it is for, say, the DVLA to translate the driving licence into Welsh, it is a *different kind* of task, and quite a difficult one at that. Are the Greeks and the Romans destined to be hidden from us for ever behind a veil of semi-incomprehension?

The most basic and difficult problem with translating ancient texts is that we still don't know what some words actually *mean*. This is the case, for example, with various words denoting plants and animals. In some instances, matters are complicated by the fact that words can mean more than one thing. The Greek words *ailouros* and *galé* and the Latin word *feles* can, and often do, mean "cat"; but they may sometimes also refer to other animals, such as the weasel. We are faced with this kind of direct obstacle to translation in thankfully few cases – we know with a high degree of confidence what most Latin and Greek words mean – but problems of this sort should serve as a reminder that the ancient world is still quite opaque to us in some respects.

The next problem is where we know what the individual words mean but we don't know what the classical author was trying to *say*. This is a problem in a surprisingly large number of cases. Some classical authors wrote in a deliberately complex and cryptic style. A good example of this is the historian Thucydides, who was found difficult to understand even by other ancient Greeks. But the problem isn't confined to awkward customers like Thucydides. This can be illustrated by an example from Virgil, a writer who doesn't in general have a reputation for being particularly hard to translate. In Book 1 of Virgil's *Aeneid*, the Trojan hero Aeneas arrives in the city of Carthage in north Africa. While he is wandering around, he sees murals depicting the Trojan War, which he has just escaped from:*"sunt lacrimae rerum"*, he exclaims (1.462). These are simple Latin words, and a GCSE student could translate them literally: "there are tears of things". But what was Virgil *getting* at? Some think that Aeneas is thankful for evidence that the locals have pity for the plight of the Trojans: "they have tears for these things". Others see it as a gnomic statement about the human condition: "there are tears in human affairs". Others again see it as a declaration of cosmic sympathy: "the world/universe has tears for us". It just isn't clear what Virgil meant. Maybe he didn't intend it to be.

Moving on, it is at this point that we start getting into deeper levels of translation – translation from one *culture* to another. Take a line from the Roman writer Suetonius' popular biographies of the Roman emperors. In his account of the death of the Emperor Claudius, he uses the phrase *"in numerum deorum relatus"*, "he was added to the number of the gods" (*De Vita Caesarum*, "Claudius", 45). This means that the deceased emperor was officially deified, in accordance with the established procedures of Roman state religion. Philemon Holland's 1606 translation renders the phrase as "canonized he was a saint in heaven". The canonisation of a saint was the nearest ceremony in Christian culture to the very alien phenomenon that Suetonius was describing, but clearly Claudius was not *actually* "canonized", nor was he venerated as a "saint". Is a translator entitled to take this kind of liberty with his source text in the interests of making it easier for his audience to understand? Your answer is as valid as mine.

The issues at stake in translating an ancient text are brought out particularly clearly when the text in question is a piece of poetry. The American poet Robert Frost once said famously that poetry is what gets lost in translation. We can illustrate what he meant by taking, as a test case, the opening lines of the *Odyssey*. This is the fairly literal translation that I gave in Chapter 2:

> Tell, Muse, of the many-turning man, who wandered far
> when he had sacked the sacred citadel of Troy:
> many were the men he met and the cities he saw,
> many the woes he suffered at sea in his heart,

trying to save his life and bring back his comrades.

What have professional translators and poets made of these lines? Let's start with the great British poet Alexander Pope. Pope published a famous translation of the *Odyssey*, which was partly ghost-written by a couple of less eminent poets, back in 1726. It was perhaps the second major English translation of the epic, the first being the 1614 version of George Chapman, who inspired Keats' sonnet "On Looking into Chapman's Homer". This is how Pope (or rather, his ghost-writer Elijah Fenton) began his version:

> The man for wisdom's various arts renown'd,
> Long exercised in woes, O Muse! resound;
> Who, when his arms had wrought the destined fall
> Of sacred Troy, and razed her heaven-built wall,
> Wandering from clime to clime, observant stray'd,
> Their manners noted, and their states survey'd,
> On stormy seas unnumber'd toils he bore,
> Safe with his friends to gain his natal shore.

This has the language and feel of a heroic epic. The iambic pentameter used by Pope is arguably the nearest native English equivalent to the Greek epic metre used by Homer, the dactylic hexameter. In the same way, rhyme is a conventional mark of English poetry. Pope's version looks and sounds properly poetic in the same way that Homer's text would have looked and sounded poetic to a Greek. As far as verbal accuracy is concerned, however, Pope is taking quite a few liberties. In the Greek – to take just a few examples – Troy's fall is not "destined", there is no mention of her wall, the seas crossed by Odysseus are not "stormy" and his shore is not "natal". A Greek epic has been rendered into something like an English epic, but at the cost of losing strict accuracy at the textual level. I will say, however, that Pope's translation does have the rare distinction amongst English versions of putting the key word "man" at the start (or as close to the start as the English language will allow).

Many modern readers know the *Odyssey* through E.V. Rieu's translation, which is a minor English literary classic in its own right. It was originally published in 1946 as the first book in the Penguin Classics series, and it was subsequently republished in a revised edition in 1991. This is what Rieu does with the opening lines:

Tell me, Muse, the story of that resourceful man who was driven to wander far and wide after he had sacked the holy citadel of Troy. He saw the cities of many people and he learnt their ways. He suffered great anguish on the high seas in his struggles to preserve his life and bring his comrades home.

Rieu's translation probably remains the most gentle introduction to Homer for the general reader, but it doesn't really capture the spirit and mood of the original Greek poetry. This is not just because Rieu is writing in prose, although that certainly doesn't help. Rieu is happy to use English idioms like "far and wide" and "high seas" which aren't quite faithful to the Greek. In more general terms, the voice that speaks to us is that of an English classicist of the 1940s rather than that of an archaic Greek bard. Rieu has done more to make Homer known to a modern English audience than any other modern translator; but we might wonder how far his popularity is due to him shielding his readers from the full archaic Greekness of Homer rather than exposing them to it.

These days, a new translation of the *Odyssey* is published every couple of years. One good example of a high-profile contemporary translation is that of the late American scholar Robert Fagles (1996). This was what Fagles made of Homer:

Sing to me of the man, Muse, the man of twists and turns

driven time and again off course, once he had plundered
the hallowed heights of Troy.
Many cities of men he saw and learned their minds,
many pains he suffered, heartsick on the open sea,
fighting to save his life and bring his comrades home.

Fagles certainly gets one thing right. His versification may not follow an orthodox English metre like Pope's, but it gets about as close to the general feel of the Greek epic hexameter as is possible in English. By his own account, Fagles was aiming for something between the Greek hexameter and a natural English metre, and I would be inclined to say that he succeeded. As to the text, Fagles is capable of being quite literal: "Many cities of men he saw and learned their minds" is pretty close to the original Greek, for instance. At times, however, Fagles the poet is at some risk of intruding on Homer the poet. Some idioms are as Fagelian as they are Homeric: "the man of twists and turns", "heartsick on the open sea".

The final translation I want to look at is that of Rodney Merrill (2002). The distinguishing feature of Merrill's *Odyssey* is that it is composed in the same hexameter metre as Homer's original text. It therefore gives us some idea of what Homer's lines originally sounded like:

> Tell me, Muse, of the man versatile and resourceful, who wandered
> many a sea-mile after he ransacked Troy's holy city.
> Many the men whose towns he observed, whose minds he discovered,
> many the pains in his heart he suffered, traversing the seaway,
> fighting for his own life and a way back home for his comrades.

Merrill was not the first to try translating Homer into English hexameters, but his rendition is a major achievement. It apparently took him a quarter of a century to complete. In my view, however, it just goes to show that hexameters don't really work in English. The metre inherently fits less easily with the English language than it does with the very different rhythms and structure of Greek. Accordingly, while Merrill's translation is generally close to the original, one suspects that he is sometimes filling out the line to make up the metre ("versatile and resourceful", "traversing the seaway"). Of course, you may disagree and think it's wonderful. If so, you may be interested to know that Merrill recorded an audio book of his translation (just as Sir Ian McKellen recorded Fagles' version).

*

I hope we can all agree that literature is very important. But for many people some things are more important still. What if a translation problem arises over the *most* important thing in the world? What if it arises over something *sacred?* Struggles over issues of language and translation often arise in religious contexts. They have arisen in the Church of England over the archaic English of the King James Bible and the Book of Common Prayer. They have arisen in the Jewish faith over the continuing use of Hebrew. They have arisen over the translation of the Qur'an, which devout Muslims believe cannot *be* adequately translated from Arabic. They have arisen in the Eastern Orthodox Churches. In 1901, an attempt by Queen Olga of Greece, a devout Orthodox Christian, to promote a translation of the ancient Greek Bible into modern Greek led to riots in the streets and the fall of the government. More recently, there have been controversies between liberal and conservative biblical scholars over how to interpret the Greek text of the New Testament in the passages which are said to condemn homosexuality. Whether a person's sexual orientation is accepted and affirmed or rejected and condemned can hinge on the precise connotations that are ascribed to the words *arsenokoités* and *malakos.*

I started with Molesworth, but not every modern Latin-speaker learns the language at a minor public school. Even today, a few learn it as altar boys in the more conservative parishes of the Roman Catholic Church. Church Latin was originally an ecumenical matter – until the 17th century, it was the language of Protestantism as well as Catholicism. As recently as the 1960s, Catholics were still using Latin for all sorts of purposes, not only for official Vatican business and theological disquisitions, but also for daily public worship in parishes throughout the Catholic world, from Vietnam to Ireland. Latin was enshrined as the language of the most important and iconic ceremony of the Catholic faith – the sacred ritual of the Mass, in which Jesus Christ himself is believed to become present on the altar in the physical form of bread and wine.

The arguments used by Catholics to justify the continuing ecclesiastical use of Latin are interesting in themselves. They should be particularly interesting to the secular reader who is looking for an insight into the mind of a devout believer, and they should banish any lingering notion that translation is an essentially technical matter without wider psychological and cultural implications. Here is a purple passage from the writings of a German priest, Fr Nicholas Gihr:

In the unchangeableness of the Latin for divine worship the Roman Missal [Mass book] appears as an intangible and inviolable sanctuary, deserving of admiration and profound respect. Since the Latin language has been withdrawn from daily life, from the ordinary intercourse of mankind, since it is not heard on the street or in the market-place, it possesses in the eyes of the faithful a holy, venerable, mystic character.... The celebration of [the Mass] fittingly calls for a language elevated, majestic, dignified and consecrated; religious sentiment demands this, and the Latin tongue answers this requirement.... The majesty of the divine worship depends, indeed, chiefly on the devout, dignified and reverential demeanour of the celebrant; but the liturgical language contributes also its share thereunto, and a foreign language is suitable, in a measure, to veil the defects and repulsive routine of many a priest, and to prevent them from appearing so glaring. (*The Holy Sacrifice of the Mass* (St Louis: Herder, 1908), 324-325)

In some ways, this reverence for the Latin language conceals more than it reveals. The Latin of the Catholic liturgy was not the polished classical Latin of Virgil and Livy – it was, at least in part, the Latin of the street. At the high point of the Mass, when the priest pronounces the words of Jesus Christ, "Take this and eat it, all of you; for this is my body", the word used for "eat" is not the classical *edete* but the colloquial *manducate*. Christ is represented as saying something like "munch on this". Indeed, Latin was originally adopted as a liturgical language because worshippers in western Europe no longer understood Greek: as the *lingua franca* of the Roman Empire, Greek had been the original operating language of the Christian church.

What happens when you take away the status of a sacred language and start to celebrate religious rites in a profane tongue? This is what has happened in the Catholic world in recent decades. The Church went through a modernisation process following the Second Vatican Council (1962-65), and by the 1970s the old Latin Mass had been replaced with a revised liturgy which is almost always celebrated in modern languages. The long-lived Pope John Paul II was almost completely uninterested in Latin (and indeed in liturgy in general, as many of his papal Masses demonstrated). The language was rehabilitated to some extent under Benedict XVI, who *was* interested in liturgy – but even Benedict, for all his conservative leanings, made no attempt to bring about a general Latin revival. Pope Francis doesn't seem to have much time for Latin at all. Encyclicals are still officially promulgated in the language, but everyone knows that they are drafted in Italian, and Vatican-watchers accordingly treat the Italian text as definitive (perhaps they will now have to shift to Spanish).

How did the world's Catholics react to the switch away from Latin? Some simply refused to go along with it. A small minority of priests and their congregations continued to use the old Latin rites; this ultra-traditionalist faction effectively turned the language into a symbol of defiance against the reforms of the Second Vatican Council. A much larger number of conservative priests switched over to the reformed rituals, with varying degrees of enthusiasm; yet they and their successors still continue to throw in some Latin prayers and to wheel out the old Latin Mass once in a while.

This brings us on to an interesting controversy, which illustrates some of the problems with translation which we have been looking at – problems which beset the academic scholar of the classical world as much as the devout Catholic. When the Mass was translated into English in the 1970s, by a body called ICEL, enormous controversy resulted. It is easiest to explain why with an example. The beginning of the oldest and most sacred prayer in the Mass, the Roman Canon (also known as "Eucharistic Prayer I"), runs as follows:

Te igitur, clementissime Pater, per Jesum Christum filium tuum Dominum nostrum, supplices rogamus ac petimus: uti accepta habeas et benedicas haec dona, haec munera, haec sancta sacrificia illibata....

The current official ICEL translation, which was introduced in 2010, tells us well enough what this literally means:

To you, therefore, most merciful Father, we make humble prayer and petition through Jesus Christ, your Son, our Lord: that you accept and bless these gifts, these offerings, these holy and unblemished sacrifices....

Between 1973 and 2010, however, worshippers in the English-speaking world heard the priest say these words:

We come to you, Father, with praise and thanksgiving, through Jesus Christ your Son. Through him we ask you to accept and bless these gifts we offer you in sacrifice....

This is not so much a translation as a loose paraphrase. God is no longer "most merciful" and Jesus Christ is no longer "our Lord". There is mention of "praise and thanksgiving" – worthy notions, no doubt, but not notions that are found anywhere in the Latin text. The second half of the passage reduces two Latin verbs (*"rogamus et petimus"*) to one English verb ("ask") and two Latin noun phrases (*"haec dona, haec munera"*) to one English noun phrase ("these gifts"); and the gifts are no longer "holy" or "unblemished".

This is the sort of thing that ICEL did throughout the 1973 translation of the Mass. For some, the effect was to give Catholic worship a new simplicity and ease of understanding for ordinary people after centuries of Latinate obscurity. Others found the translation to be patronising, ugly and filled with mistakes. When the more accurate, but rather stilted, translation came along in 2010, the whole acrimonious dispute was reignited. It will be a long time before it dies down again. At stake is not just the technocratic question of how to translate from one language into another – can we render *"haec dona, haec munera"* as "these gifts" – is it pedantic to insist on "these gifts, these offerings"? We also have the problem of how to translate from one culture into another – from the dying days of imperial Rome to 21st century Dublin and Los Angeles. Do we preserve the rhythms and rhetoric of the original text, or do we go for a more contemporary feel? Finally, for Catholics, there is a third, theological consideration – is God a King who is to be addressed in courtly language or a Father who can be spoken to easily and informally? It is not a coincidence that the 1973 translation was adopted under a relatively liberal pope, Paul VI, while the 2010 translation was adopted under a more conservative pontiff, Benedict XVI. Translation can be a matter of ideology and politics as much as grammar and syntax.

*

So much for translation; now for some history. Where did the classical languages *come* from? We can follow the trail surprisingly far back into the gloom of prehistory.

We can pick up the trail by looking for the earliest traces of the Greek language – Greek rather than Latin, because Latin is a rather young language by comparison. The ancestors of the Greeks may have come to Greece in, very roughly, the last few centuries of the 3rd millennium BC. As is noted in the list of historical periods in Chapter 1, the first known Greek civilisation was the Mycenaean culture, named after the city of Mycenae in central Greece. The Mycenaeans are famous for their monumental palaces. They flourished in roughly the second half of the 2nd millennium BC; the exact dates are subject to debate. Note that this was long before anyone had heard of Rome. The only earlier civilisation in the region was the older "Minoan" culture on the island of Crete. Little is known about the Minoans, who had a non-Greek language and culture, but much has been fantasised about them. Some modern writers have given in to a temptation to see Minoan society as a pacifist, feminist utopia, which is a pleasing idea but not especially plausible. They painted pretty pictures, at least. These pictures, along with other Minoan remains, were imaginatively restored by Sir Arthur Evans, the British archaeologist who first dug them up. He took some liberties in the process, one famous example being a "restored" picture of a boy gathering flowers which later turned out to have originally been a picture of a blue monkey. Evans' endeavours are a good example of how the ancient world can end up being creatively refashioned, or distorted, when modern people come to grips with it.

We know that the Mycenaeans were Greeks because they helpfully left behind administrative records in an early form of the Greek language, written in a bizarre script known as Linear B. This is the start of the written history of Greek. (If you're wondering what Linear *A* was, it was the script of the Minoans – it has still not been deciphered, but everyone agrees that the underlying language isn't Greek. Trying to guess what it *is* has become something of a parlour game among scholars of Mediterranean prehistory.) What the Mycenaeans *didn't* leave behind was anything resembling literature – we have to wait for

Homer for that. For reasons which are still not entirely clear, Mycenaean civilisation had collapsed by the end of the 2nd millennium BC, and Greek culture entered the "Dark Age" which we have already come across. There is still much that we don't know about these developments. Ancient history can be a very murky business.

Where did the Greeks themselves come from? For many scholars over the last couple of hundred years, the answer to this question would have been obvious. The origins of the Greeks lay in *Indo-European* society, and the Greeks came to Greece from the Indo-European homeland, which was widely believed to have been in southern Russia. In order to explain who these mysterious "Indo-Europeans" were, we have to go back to the late 18th century. In 1786, a British colonial judge called Sir William Jones gave an address to the Asiatic Society in Calcutta in which he put forward the following theory:

> The Sanskrit language, whatever be its antiquity, is of a wonderful structure; more perfect than the Greek, more copious than the Latin, and more exquisitely refined than either, yet bearing to both of them a stronger affinity, both in the roots of verbs and in the forms of grammar, than could possibly have been produced by accident; so

strong indeed, that no philologer could examine them all three, without believing them to have sprung from some common source, which, perhaps, no longer exists: there is a similar reason, though not quite so forcible, for supposing that both the Gothic and the Celtic, though blended with a very different idiom, had the same origin with the Sanskrit; and the old Persian might be added to the same family....

Jones was not the first to come up with this idea of a "common source" for the languages of Europe and western Asia, but he is usually given the credit for doing so. In any event, this insight gave birth to the discipline of "Indo-European" studies. It is now pretty certain that the Indo-European languages, which include every language in Europe except a few oddities like Finnish and Basque, are related in some way (although experts, who are paid to argue about this stuff, argue endlessly about exactly how and why these interrelationships developed). The hypothetical "common source" of which Jones spoke is generally now known as Proto-Indo-European, or PIE for short.

Reconstructing PIE is fairly simple, at least in principle. The Latin word for "father" is *pater*. The Greek word is, likewise, *patér*. If we look further east, the Sanskrit word is *pita*.

If we look to the barbarian north, the Anglo-Saxon word was *faeder*. It is reasonable to conclude that there is some older word underlying all these terms which must have been used by the ancestors of the Romans, Greeks, Indians and Anglo-Saxons. Scholars think that it was something like *p-h-tér* (the *-h-* represents a sound called a laryngeal – don't even ask). The same trick can be repeated with numerous other words, allowing us to build up a whole reconstructed lexicon for PIE. Of course, there is a fair amount of guesswork involved here, and we can't exactly check with the Indo-Europeans whether or not our reconstructions are accurate; but we can reconstruct quite an extensive corpus of PIE terms with at least some degree of confidence.

Once PIE had begun to be reconstructed by 19th century scholars, the temptation grew to reconstruct an ancestral Indo-European culture to go with it. This was a much more ambitious project, with some interesting implications. Reconstructed words for gods, farm produce, family relationships and so on enabled researchers to reconstruct various aspects of the social world of the mysterious prehistoric people who had spoken PIE. If an object or a concept had a reconstructible name in PIE, it must by definition have been known to the speakers of PIE and so probably formed part of their society. For example, PIE had reconstructible words for "cattle", "sheep" and "pig", so it was a fair bet that the Indo-Europeans had farmed those animals. Early texts written in Indo-European languages were also scoured for clues of what the writers' forefathers had been like. A well-known French scholar, Georges Dumézil, came up with a theory that the Indo-Europeans had recognised three social "functions" corresponding broadly to ruling, warmaking and farming. These continued to be reflected in, for example, the three leading Hindu castes of Brahmans, *Kshatriya* and *Vaishya*.

Whole shelves of books have been written about this stuff, and whole careers have been built on it. Some of it is probably even true. Somewhere along the line, however, things took a nasty turn. The idea of a pristine, primaeval Indo-European ancestor society became mixed up with fashionable ideas of racial supremacy. If the Indo-Europeans were our ancestors, they must have been pretty special people, right? Especially compared to the ancestors of, say, the black Africans. Or the Jews. It is no coincidence that the Indo-Europeans used to be referred to as the "Aryans", before that term mysteriously went out of fashion after 1945. The American scholar Bruce Lincoln has drawn attention to a crossover in more recent times between Indo-European studies and the political extreme right. The best known example of this is Dumézil and his three "functions". It was suggested (probably a little unfairly) that Dumézil's academic work on prescriptive social categories might not be wholly unrelated to his right-wing political leanings.

None of which means that Indo-European studies are inherently fascist or that present-day scholars working in the field are racial supremacists – the vast majority of them are nothing of the kind. But it does provide one explanation of why the Indo-Europeans aren't everybody's cup of tea. In more general terms, classicists have become more aware in recent years of how far scholars' prejudices have shaped orthodox views of the ancient world. One historian, Martin Bernal, wrote a massive three-volume study entitled *Black Athena*. In it, he attempted to argue that Greece was heavily indebted to African and Asian societies and that this had been covered up by 19th and 20th century scholars, mainly for racist reasons. Bernal's work generated a fierce debate, particularly in the United States, and the consensus today is that he overstated his case. Indeed, he was very honest about how his work was shaped by his own ideological agenda (Bernal was a politically active left-winger). But *Black Athena* did force classical scholars to engage with some uncomfortable truths about the past of their own profession. Bernal's work serves as a useful reminder that classical studies do not exist in a political vacuum.

Can history be traced back before the Indo-Europeans? After all, linguists have reconstructed other proto-languages around the world, such as Proto-Sino-Tibetan in eastern Asia and Proto-Semitic in the Middle East. Can we compare reconstructed terms in PIE with those in other proto-languages? Can we reconstruct Proto-World? The answer is probably "No". Bear in mind that PIE itself is only a hypothesis which is reconstructed on a best-guess basis. If we try to take the project even further back in time, things start to get silly. A few proposals for proto-proto-languages are made from time to time, but none of them has yet found wide acceptance. One example is the proposed proto-proto-language of "Nostratic", which would have extended across Europe, Asia, Africa and the Arctic.

In fact, there has been a long history of people attempting to deduce the original, primaeval language of mankind. The Greek historian Herodotus, whom we met in Chapter 1, reported that the original language was Phrygian and told a famous story about how this discovery was made. The Egyptian pharaoh Psamtik I ordered that two children should be brought up without being exposed to human speech, in the hope that they would spontaneously start speaking the original language. They ended up coming up with the word *"bekos"*, which turned out to be Phrygian for "bread". So Phrygian, it seemed, was the prototypical human language. Later on, in the Christian era, Hebrew was always a strong candidate for a proto-language because of its biblical credentials, but powerful representations were made on behalf of other languages too, including such counter-intuitive candidates as Irish and Dutch. For more information on this strange corner of intellectual history, readers are referred to Umberto Eco's book *The Search for the Perfect Language*.

4. Gender, Sexuality and Satire by a Conservative

Gender and sexuality are particularly slippery areas for the historian. This is because they are made up of a combination of innate human desires mixed in with rules and customs which vary widely between different societies. The fact that *some* attitudes and behaviours are instantly familiar can blind us to the unfamiliarity of others. For example, the poet Ovid wrote two books of light-hearted advice for young men on how to pick up girls, plus a further book for girls on how to get a man – this was *The Art of Love*, the work which is said to have offended the Emperor Augustus. Some of Ovid's dating advice sounds remarkably modern – the best place to pick up partners, personal hygiene, how to make your boyfriend jealous. It has duly been repackaged for modern readers by Charlotte Higgins in a witty little book called *Latin Love Lessons*, which I recommend to interested readers. Yet similarities of this sort can be deceptive. In other respects, ancient attitudes to relationships and sexual behaviour differed greatly from ours.

A good example of this is homosexuality (by which I mean *male* homosexuality – we have much less evidence about lesbianism). It is well known that the Greeks and the Romans had no general moral objection to same-sex liaisons. As early as Homer, we have what may well be a homoerotic relationship between Achilles and his beloved companion Patroclus in the *Iliad*, although Homer is not quite clear about whether the two men are actually sleeping together. Centuries later, in the 100s AD, the Roman Empire was showered with statues, coins, temples and cities named in honour of the Emperor Hadrian's deceased lover Antinous, whom Hadrian had declared to be a god. Between these two points (and after them), there was a consistent tradition of same-sex love and eroticism which can easily be found in ancient literature and the archaeological record. Seen from this perspective, it might be tempting to see the Greeks and the Romans as early gay rights advocates.

That, however, would be a mistake. Graeco-Roman society had no general, overarching concept of committed same-sex relationships between adults. Such relationships did exist – indeed, it has been argued that some parts of the ancient world had something approximating to same-sex marriages. But it would be unwise to assume that modern-style relationships of this sort were the norm for ancient homosexuality. The archetypal form of homosexual behaviour in the Greek world was "pederasty", or *paiderasteia* – a short-term liaison between an adult male and an adolescent youth. This kind of arrangement was symbolised by the legend of Zeus abducting Ganymede, a handsome Trojan boy, to serve as his cup-bearer. The Romans, who were never really as enthusiastic as the Greeks about this sort of thing, were even more prescriptive. They insisted that the youth be a slave or a prostitute rather than a freeborn citizen boy. Exactly where the custom of pederasty came from has been debated. It seems to be quite common in pre-industrial societies. It is sometimes said that it originated from archaic initiation rites in which the older males of the community initiated boys into manhood through sexual practices, but this is difficult to prove. The practice also seems to have had links with the élite culture of Greek aristocrats.

This stuff can be quite difficult for us to get our heads around. If there is one form of sexual behaviour that remains utterly stigmatised in the modern world, it is paedophilia, and the ancient Greeks and Romans look a bit too much like paedos for comfort. What is more, one influential current within classical studies, led by the English classicist Sir Kenneth Dover and the French philosopher Michel Foucault, has seen ancient pederasty as forming part of a broader web of social relations of domination and humiliation. This is clearly a long way from *Will and Grace*.

It is only fair to say that other scholars have argued that Dover and Foucault went too far, and that ancient pederasty did not in fact amount to child abuse. This point of view has been championed in recent years by, amongst others, James Davidson of Warwick University. In Athens, for example, it is argued that men were only supposed to begin physical relationships with youths when the latter reached 18, the age of citizenship. Even if this is true, however, it shouldn't entirely dispel our unease: puberty occurred later in the ancient world, and an 18-year-old youth would have been equivalent in terms of sexual maturity to a modern 14-year-old. More generally, whatever the accepted protocols were, there isn't much evidence that the Greeks or Romans saw anything wrong with the disparity of maturity and power that would have characterised pederastic relationships. Some ancient writers, notably Plato, seem to have been uncomfortable with this aspect of their culture, but Plato was not necessarily clear or consistent on this point, and in any case he had a more general suspicion of the physical side of sexuality. Indeed, it was Plato's views in this area that gave rise to the concept of "Platonic" relationships.

Another reason why the Greeks and Romans would not have been queuing up to join Stonewall is that they had something very similar to our own society's traditional prejudice against effeminate men. Whatever might have been the case with boys and youths, it was considered a disgrace for a grown adult male to engage in passive sexual behaviour or otherwise to assimilate himself to a woman. Such a man was reviled as a *kinaidos* (Greek) or *cinaedus* (Latin). This prejudice would have helped to stop adult gay couples from developing as a widespread social norm. Allegations of femininity were used as insults, and could have serious consequences if the target chose to avenge the slight to his manhood. In democratic Athens, the politician Cleisthenes was pilloried by the comic playwright Aristophanes for being effeminate. Periander, the dictator of Corinth, is said to have been killed by his outraged boy-lover when he jokingly asked the latter whether he was pregnant yet.

This leads us on to a broader point about ideas of femininity and the role of women. It will come as no surprise to discover that the ancient world was not a hospitable place for women's rights and feminism. This was famously argued many years ago by an American classical scholar, Sarah Pomeroy, in one of those books whose title is largely self-explanatory: *Goddesses, Whores, Wives and Slaves*. At the very beginning of Greek literature, the

Iliad depicts the hero Hector instructing his wife Andromache in the proper duties of men and women:

> But go to the house and take care of your own work,
>
> the loom and the distaff, and tell the slave-girls
>
> to take up their work; war shall be the concern of all
>
> the men, those who are sons of Troy, and me above all.
>
> (*Iliad* 6.490-493)

It would be easy to pile up this kind of quotation to illustrate Graeco-Roman sexism, and indeed it would be easy to play the same game for most pre-modern societies. It may be more interesting, however, to take a closer look at some of the variations and grey areas in ancient attitudes towards gender and sexuality, and at some of their less predictable aspects.

Let's take an example. In Chapter 1, I mentioned women veiling their heads – an act which is nowadays widely interpreted by Western people as an act of oppression. Both Greek and Roman women seem to have veiled their heads in public. We find in the sources the following story about the Roman politician Gaius Sulpicius Gallus:

He divorced his wife because he had caught her outdoors with her head uncovered: a stiff penalty, but not without a certain logic. "The law," he said, "prescribes for you my eyes alone to which you may prove your beauty. For these eyes you should provide the ornaments of beauty, for these be lovely: entrust yourself to their more certain knowledge. If you, with needless provocation, invite the look of anyone else, you must be suspected of wrongdoing." (Valerius Maximus, 6.3.10; trans. M.R.Lefkowitz and M.B.Fant)

Can we conclude from this that the Romans' attitude towards female dress was no different from, say, that of the Taliban? Probably not. Mary Beard has pointed out that this passage appears in a collection of examples of how tough old Romans used to behave. The original audience of the anecdote was not supposed to find it typical of their own culture – they were supposed to be surprised (and impressed) by the contrast between their own laxity and the higher standards supposedly observed by their ancestors. It is a bit like modern stories about the Victorians covering up table legs.

Generally speaking, it looks like the status of women was somewhat higher in Rome than it was in Greece, particularly in

Athens. The Roman family-mother, or *materfamilias*, could be a formidable character, more tiger mother than little wifey. By contrast, some scholars have portrayed Athens as a highly repressive patriarchal culture. In addition to wearing veils, women were confined to certain parts of the house, and the etiquette among men was not to refer to each other's women by name – they were simply "the wife of Thucydides", or whatever. In some cases, scholars have overtly approved of such arrangements:

> ....[C]onversation with men, such as highly cultivated Athenians demanded as their daily bread, was impossible for women, considering their entirely different psychological conditions and their completely different interests – it was this that banished the woman to the seclusion of the woman's chamber. (Hans Licht, *Sexual Life in Ancient Greece* (London: Routledge, 2009), 38; Licht, whose real name was Paul Brandt, was writing in the 1920s)

In the eyes of other scholars, Athenian men abused their women and treated them with contempt. This interpretation of Athenian society was famously put forward in another book by an

American feminist with a highly suggestive title, *The Reign of the Phallus* by Eva Keuls. Keuls seems to have been deliberately trying to shock her readers into seeing what she considered to be the miasma of repression and rape behind Athenian high culture. Yet she achieved this effect at the expense of reading her sources in a very tendentious and misleading way. Even architectural pillars get pressed into her argument as symbols of phallic domination. We are reminded once again that what we make of the historical evidence is likely to be coloured by the presuppositions that we ourselves bring to the table.

The social position of women varied considerably not merely between Greece and Rome but also within those societies. Even if Keuls was exaggerating, women in Athens do seem to have been rather closely controlled, whereas women in Sparta had a higher status. Aristotle, whose views on these matters were notoriously sexist, complained about this and referred to Sparta as a "gynaecocracy" or "regime of women" (*Politics*, 1269b-1270a). Gender differences were certainly less pronounced at Sparta than at Athens, and women could freely divorce their husbands and own property – a right which was denied to married women in England until 1870. Even within a single *polis*, the position of women must have varied a lot. It may be that the Athenian norm of anonymous, segregated women was confined in practice to the higher, more "respectable" social classes. The average small farmer trying to make a living from the land probably couldn't afford to have his wife sitting in a back room of the house all day.

These days, a trip to any reasonably well stocked bookshop will reveal countless pop psychology and self-help books arguing about whether male and female behaviour is all in the genes or whether it is shaped by cultural norms – the nature/nurture debate. This debate was already known about, and pursued with some vigour, in classical times. Some ancient writers predictably treated gender roles as iron laws of nature, just as they regarded it as "natural" that barbarians were inherently inferior and that slaves were slaves. But it may come as a surprise to learn that some ancient writers inclined to the "nurture" side of the debate. The historian Herodotus, whom we have met a couple of times now, famously thought that "custom is king", a conclusion he supported by reference to the funerary practices of different nations (*History*, 3.38). Plato was prepared to allow women into the governing class of his ideal utopian state. On a more mundane level, the Roman biographer Cornelius Nepos (c.110 – c.25 BC) had this to say:

It was no disgrace for Cimon, a highly eminent man of Athens, to marry his half-sister, since his fellow-citizens followed the same custom. Yet this is considered an outrage by our standards. In Crete it is thought praiseworthy for young men to have as many boyfriends as possible.... Conversely, many things are held to be fitting by our standards whereas they are thought disgraceful by the Greeks. What Roman feels shame in taking his wife to a banquet? What *materfamilias* does not live in the best part of the house and mix with company? Such things are done very differently in Greece. A woman is not admitted to a banquet except among relatives, and she is confined to the inner part of the house, which is called the "women's quarters"; no-one is allowed in there except close male relatives. (*De Viris Illustribus*, Preface)

Some things may differ between societies, but other things never change, and one of those is the prevalence of the world's oldest profession. The ancient world had a thriving sex industry. At one end of the scale, we know of Belle de Jour-type high-class escorts, whom the Greeks euphemistically called *hetairai*, "companions". The Athenian statesman Pericles had a long-term partner, Aspasia, who may have been a *hetaira*. Some ancient sources present *hetairai* as witty, educated, charming vixens, and some modern writers have accepted this portrayal. For their part, feminist scholars have suggested that this may be a projection of the male writers' own fantasies. At any rate, some *hetairai* became wealthy and achieved something like celebrity status, a bit like modern actresses or supermodels:

> Phryne was very rich and promised to build a wall around Thebes if the Thebans wrote on it: "Alexander [the Great] destroyed this wall, but Phryne the *hetaira* rebuilt it." Callistratus recounts this in his *On Hetairai*. (Athenaeus, 944a)

Of course, it is significant in itself that a writer would write and publish a book entitled *On Hetairai*. It is a great shame that the rest of it has been lost.

At the other end of the scale, there were the less fortunate girls, often slaves, who worked for pimps in brothels (*pornai*, the origin of our "porn-" words). There is even evidence that the semi-legendary Athenian lawgiver Solon established state-run brothels:

> Seeing the city was full of young men,
> who had natural urges

AN INTRODUCTION TO CLASSICS

and were straying where they shouldn't,

he bought women, put them in brothels,

and made them ready for common use.

They're naked. No-one's pretending. Have a good look....

....The door's open.

One obol [a unit of currency]. Go in! There's no

prudery, no crap, no deceit –

just do what you want, however you want.

Then go – tell her to piss off. She's nothing to you.

(Philemon at Athenaeus, 569e-f)

Note that this is a speech from an otherwise lost comic play, so we don't know how seriously it was supposed to be taken or how typical such attitudes were. It might be the ancient equivalent of a piece of dialogue from *Men Behaving Badly*. A more ambivalent attitude towards the sex industry is found in this anecdote about the stern old Roman statesman Cato the Elder (234 – 149 BC), whose ideas about correct moral behaviour were considered strict even by Roman standards:

As Cato was passing, a man walked out of a brothel. He hurried away from Cato, but Cato called him back and praised him. Later, when Cato saw him leaving the same brothel more frequently, he is said to have told him: "Young man, I praised you for coming here sometimes, not for living here." (Ps.-Acro, Commentary on Horace, *Satires* 1.2)

This needs to be unpacked a bit. When Cato praised the young man, he had a moral motivation: the youth was doing right by resorting to prostitutes for sexual gratification rather than seducing respectable girls (in other words, the daughters of men like Cato). This, incidentally, is also what the reference to "straying where they shouldn't" meant in the previous passage. But the frequency of the young man's visits suggested that he was indulging his appetites too freely – which was equally unacceptable behaviour for a self-respecting Roman man.

So much for the sex industry. What about conventional marriage? There is a temptation to see ancient marriage as a grim, loveless business – an arrangement made between the couple's parents for reasons of family politics and in order to ensure that property was passed down to legitimate children. Until quite recently, it was considered good form among scholars to claim that of course "love" in the romantic sense didn't even exist as a concept until it was invented by the *troubadours* of mediaeval France, with their songs about chivalrous courtly love.

There is some degree of truth in all this. People in the ancient world didn't tend to marry, first and foremost, for love. They did so in conformity with social custom and out of obedience to their parents, and also in order to have children. We find in our sources the predictable take-my-wife-please cynicism about marriage and wives that we find among men in many societies. When the Roman grandee Quintus Metellus gave a speech encouraging men to marry, he was criticised for talking about the "nuisance and endless inconveniences" of married life. His defenders replied that it was more important for a man in his position to tell the truth, "especially when he was speaking about a matter which was widely understood through everyday knowledge and common, shared life experience" (Aulus Gellius, 1.6.3).

Yet ancient marriage cannot be properly understood without looking at the emotional content of the relationships between husbands and wives. Ethnographic research has shown that romantic love is not a cultural oddity from mediaeval France or 21st century Hollywood, and it should come as no surprise to find that it existed in classical antiquity. Indeed, it was seen as a natural and desirable part of the marriage relationship. Right back in archaic times, the *Odyssey* offers us a model of marriage which remains inspiring and moving today – a couple who are both intellectually matched and deeply in love with one another. In later periods, the idea of marriage as a love match came to be a standard theme in the plots of comic plays by writers like Menander (in Greece) and Plautus and Terence (in Rome). The same sort of link between marriage and romantic love also appears in ancient novels – not many people realise that the Greeks and the Romans invented pulp fiction. People in the ancient world may have married for a variety of reasons and had a variety of experiences within marriage; but it clearly wasn't *all* about money and family alliances. The Greeks and the Romans themselves certainly didn't think so.

Even in sources which display very prescriptive and sexist attitudes, we can find some evidence of men viewing marriage as a joint endeavour between the husband and wife. The following fictional dialogue appears in a work by the Greek writer Xenophon (c.430 – c.350 BC), who was on the whole a decidedly conservative sort of chap. It is worth quoting at some length because of its curious mixture of very traditional and surprisingly enlightened views:

SOCRATES: I would very much like to learn this from you, Ischomachus – did you yourself train your wife to be as she needed to be, or did she already know how to accomplish the duties that belonged to her when you took her from her father and mother?

ISCHOMACHUS: Now, Socrates, how could she have known such things when I took her? She was not yet 15 years old when she came to me, and throughout her life up to then she had been brought up with great care so that she saw as little as possible, heard as little as possible and asked as little as possible. Don't you think it's acceptable if she came knowing only how to take wool and make a dress, and that she had learned how the wool-spinning duties were to be allocated among the slave-girls?...

Why, Socrates, when I had brought her under control and she was sufficiently domesticated to talk with me, I asked her this: "Tell me, my wife, have you ever thought about why I chose you and your parents gave you to me?... It was because I was minded to find for my own sake, as your parents were for your sake, the best possible partner for my house and children.... And so, if the gods ever give us children, we will take decisions about them together, so that we bring them up in the best way possible.... At present, however, we have this house in common, since I am putting everything which I possess into our common resources, as you have put all of your dowry into our common resources. And we need not calculate which of us has contributed more in value: we need only know that whichever of us contributes what is most worth having is the better partner." (*Economics*, 7)

Again, a modern audience will probably be wondering what kind of sicko would marry a 14-year-old girl, but an ancient audience would have been more likely to be struck by the fact that Ischomachus was prepared to see his wife as being an equal partner in any sense at all.

Comparable sentiments from the Roman world can be found in the teachings of a highly influential philosopher called Musonius Rufus. Musonius accepted the traditional view that marriage was for childrearing, but he insisted that it was also about an interpersonal union:

The husband and wife... should come together for the purpose of making a life in common and of procreating children, and furthermore of regarding all things in common between them, and nothing peculiar or private to one or the other.... [I]n marriage there must be above all perfect companionship and mutual love of husband and wife, both in health and in sickness and under all conditions, since it was with desire for this as well as for having children that both entered upon marriage. Where, then, this love for each other is perfect and the two share it completely, each striving to outdo the other in devotion, the marriage is ideal and worthy of envy, for such a union is beautiful.... Therefore those who contemplate marriage ought to have regard neither for family, whether either one be of high-born parents, nor for wealth, whether on either side there be great possessions, nor for physical traits, whether one or the other have beauty.... For without sympathy of mind and character between husband and wife, what marriage can be good, what partnership advantageous? (*Lectures*, 13; trans. Cora E. Lutz)

It's not exactly *Spare Rib*, but it does go further than we might expect. Even austere old Roman philosophers were prepared to depict marriage as something approaching a partnership of equals, with important psychological and emotional dimensions.

*

One place where we can find *real* sexism, together with a dislike of effeminacy and other sexually unconventional behaviour, is in the poems of a well-known Roman writer called Juvenal (c.55 – c.127 AD). Juvenal was a conservative satirist whose caustic brand of humour went on to influence writers from Ben Jonson to Jonathan Swift to Aldous Huxley. He has quite a distinctive literary style. At best, it is witty, if a little artificial. It can be dense, fast-paced, even cryptic, and peppered with allusions which modern readers – even classical scholars – cannot easily understand.

Juvenal's notorious *Satire* 6 is an extended diatribe against women – a nasty little poem which is not rescued by its acerbic wit. Why, asks Juvenal, would you get married when you can kill yourself instead? Or, for that matter, when you can sleep with a boy? Juvenal complains that women are lacking in chastity and are inclined to be unfaithful. He also accuses them of being demanding and argumentative. Nor are these the only accusations. It also turns out that women are – amongst other things – superstitious, cruel, extravagant, over-talkative, malicious, gossipy and too fond of make-up. How had women come to be so out of control? For Juvenal, the answer lay in the soft weakness of modern Roman culture, the product of years of peace and prosperity. This is a typical example of the motif of declining social standards that we find so frequently in Roman literature. Juvenal himself had something of an ascetic streak, and he repeatedly returned to the themes of avarice and luxury in his writing.

Satire 6 is particularly famous for the tag *"quis custodiet ipsos custodes?"*, "who will guard the guards themselves?". This appears in the following passage:

> ....I know
> well your advice and your warnings, my old friends:
> "Lock the door and keep her in." But who will guard the
> guards themselves? The loose girl bribes them with her favours
> and seals their lips. They are silenced by their common crime.
> The prudent wife plans this and begins her sport with them.
> The highest and the lowest have the same libido;
> she who pounds the pavements with dirty feet is no
> better than she who is carried by Syrian slaves. (O29-351)

In line with the widespread prejudice which we met earlier, Juvenal also lambasts effeminacy in men. According to him, this manifested itself in men wearing feminine dress and make-up, and adopting female religious practices and speech-patterns. Some effeminate men were even apparently going through mock wedding ceremonies dressed as brides. Juvenal was disgusted with such unmanly behaviour on the part of his fellow Romans. And it got worse. Not only were the Romans themselves a lost cause – even the simple barbarians whom they had conquered were succumbing to the same vices.

Immigrants were bad news too. Greek men were travelling to Rome and seducing Roman women, even the grandmothers. Meanwhile, their women were being pimped out at the Circus Maximus, the great chariot-racing venue in central Rome. It comes as no surprise to learn that Juvenal disliked foreigners just as much as he disliked everyone else. He complains that being a true-born Roman doesn't count for anything these days. Even foreign ex-slaves were humiliating honourable Roman citizens. What Juvenal says about Greek migrants is oddly similar to what later generations of nativists would say about the Irish and the Jews (surprise surprise, he didn't like Jews either). You can still feel the anger pulsing through his diatribes:

....Romans, I cannot bear
a Greek Rome – and how many of our scum are Greek!
The Orontes has flowed into the Tiber,
bringing its language, its customs, its flutes and slanting
harp-strings and its ancestral drums with it – and the
girls who are told to sell themselves at the Circus.

Down with men who like foreign whores in bright headscarves!

....This Greek comes from Sicyon, that one from Amydon,

or else Andros, Samos, Tralles or Alabanda.

They head for the Esquiline or the Viminal Hill –

the parasites of great houses, and their future lords –

quick-witted, utterly shameless, always ready with

words, more eloquent than Isaeus [a Greek orator]. Tell me,
what do

you think that man is? He has brought the lot with him:

teacher, orator, geometer, painter, trainer,

augur, rope-dancer, doctor, magician: the hungry

little Greek knows all the trades....

....

Worse, he holds nothing sacred – nothing is safe from his groin,

not the lady of the house, not the virgin daughter, not

her young fiancé, not the son, previously so chaste.

If he can't get these, he will seduce his friend's grandmother.

(3.60-66, 69-78, 109-112)

For Juvenal, it is clear that modern Roman society in general has become irretrievably decadent. He was, however, willing to find virtue in the places where social conservatives usually find it – the countryside and the past. The great Romans of history would, he insists, have been scandalised by the kinds of goings-on that he writes about. There was a time when Romans had been virtuous and content with simple living:

> Happy were our ancestors' forebears, happy was
> the time long ago when, ruled by kings and tribunes [an office
>   under the Republic],
> they saw that Rome was in need of only one jail. (3.312-314)

> ....Broken by age, men who had fought against
> Carthage or awful Pyrrhus or the Molossians' swords
> were given at last scarcely two acres for all their
> wounds; this recompense for their blood and toil
> never seemed to be less than they deserved or the
> meagre reward of an ungrateful country.... (14.161-166)

By contrast, modern-day Rome was blighted by crime, corruption and greed. Juvenal is fiercely polemical about this:

> To crime men owe their gardens, palaces, tables,
> their old silverware, the goblet with the embossed goat.
> Who can sleep for thinking of a greedy daughter-in-law's
> seducer, disgraced brides and teenage adulterers?
> Though nature resists it, anger writes my verse,
> such as it is....
> When was the horde of vices more swollen? When

did the bosom of greed lie more open? When were dice
played more brazenly?...
Which of our grandfathers built so many villas, or
dined by himself on seven courses?... (1.75-95)

Stop the world, I want to get off.... Juvenal is the authentic
voice of the reactionary through the ages, loudly condemning
modern urban depravity – whether attributable to women, sexual
deviancy or foreigners – and praising the superior virtues of rural
life and a past golden age. As is often the case with polemicists,
it is not entirely clear how much of his own propaganda he
believed. He may well have been pandering to the prejudices of
his audience. Some scholars have gone further and argued that he
is actually satirising the very attitudes that he expresses, though I
suspect that this lets him off the hook a little too easily (it smacks
of waving what the classical scholar Hugh Lloyd-Jones called
"the magic wand of irony"). In all, Juvenal can be summed up as
a more literary Simon Heffer, a more caustic Peter Hitchens or a
cleverer Richard Littlejohn. If he was alive today, he would have
a fighting chance of getting a column on the *Daily Mail*.

5. Philosophy and Religion in a World Full of Gods

If the ancient Greeks are famous for one thing above all else, it is philosophy. Even the name itself is Greek – *philo-sophia*, love of knowledge. In fact, what the Greeks understood by "philosophy" went a long way beyond the boundaries of what modern professional philosophers do. For one thing, ancient philosophy was not distinct from science. It would have been quite unremarkable for a philosopher to write works of zoology when he wasn't wondering about God, ethics and the good life. One thing that hasn't changed, however, is that philosophers were famous even back then for disagreeing about everything. The Roman statesman Cicero reports in his treatise *On the Laws* that one Roman governor of Greece, Lucius Gellius, tried to get all the philosophers of Athens to settle their disagreements once and for all; he even offered to help them out if they were having trouble.

The Western philosophical tradition is conventionally taken to have begun in earnest with the Athenian intellectual Socrates son of Sophroniscus (c.468 – 399 BC). Greek philosophy, however, is older than Socrates, dating back to the "Pre-Socratic" thinkers of the archaic period. The writings of the Pre-Socratics are largely lost. They consisted of shadowy figures such as Xenophanes, who argued that the Homeric gods were too badly behaved to be real; Empedocles, who anticipated Darwin's theory of evolution; and Thales, who thought that the world was made of water.

Socrates left no writings behind him, so we can access his teachings only through the writings of his followers – in particular, Plato and Xenophon (hence we met a passage of Xenophon involving a dialogue with Socrates in the last chapter). The picture of Socrates presented by these writers is inconsistent, and indeed Plato's works are notoriously inconsistent with each other. So we can't be sure what the historical Socrates was really like. This is known as the "Socratic Problem". Interestingly, it poses similar issues to those encountered by historians who study that other well-known ancient teacher who is known only though the writings of his followers: Rabbi Jeshua of Nazareth. We'll come back to him later.

From what we can gather from the very imperfect evidence available to us, Socrates was more interested in criticising the philosophical positions of others than in putting forward a doctrine of his own (for an accessible example of this, have a read

AN INTRODUCTION TO CLASSICS

of Plato's *Euthyphro*). His method seems to have been to play dumb, flatter his interlocutor into explaining his philosophical position, then mercilessly expose the flaws in that position, while all the time studiously avoiding putting forward any alternative system that could be attacked in the same way. If this sounds massively annoying, it's because it was. The philosopher Gary Cox has compared Socrates' passive-aggressive false naivety to that of the TV detective Columbo. An acquaintance of mine was probably closer to the truth when he remarked that Socrates "basically invented trolling".

It may come as no surprise to learn that Socrates was not a popular man. He was satirised by the comic playwright Aristophanes as an out-of-touch campus radical. He was executed by the people of Athens in 399 BC – ostensibly on the high-minded charges of impiety and corrupting the young men of Athens, but seemingly in reality for his connections with an anti-democratic clique which had briefly taken control of the city (predictably enough, he also fell out with the clique). It didn't help that, when he was found guilty and his punishment was being decided, he suggested to the jury that he be publicly honoured and given free meals for life. More jurors voted to sentence him to death than voted to convict him in the first place. There is a certain poetic truth in the scene in the *Horrible*

Histories TV series in which Socrates is shown asking his followers "Why?" in response to everything until they eventually lose their temper and force the hemlock down his throat themselves.

As for Socrates' pupil Plato (whose real name was apparently Aristocles), he left behind a voluminous collection of philosophical works which discuss a range of metaphysical, ethical, epistemological and political problems in exhaustive detail. Yet the Platonic works, which take the form of dramatic dialogues, are a bit of an enigma. In particular, Plato's use of the dialogue form continues to pose questions. Plato never appears as a character in any of his dialogues; at best, he uses other characters such as Socrates to express views that he himself appears to have held. He never goes so far as to explicitly present any point of view as his own. In surprisingly postmodern fashion, he offers us a chorus of disputing voices and leaves the rest to us. When presented with a quote from Plato, you don't merely have to try to get your head around what it's saying, you have to ask who said it and at what point in the conversation. Nor are the ideas in the dialogues consistent, although it is possible to draw out a fairly coherent body of "Platonic" thought from them. There is also a strange irony in the fact that Plato clearly disliked the literary arts, yet his dialogues are masterpieces of literature as well as philosophy.

Plato and his pupil Aristotle were the two giants of Greek philosophy. They continue to dominate our understanding of classical thought even today. They are generally seen as being quite different characters – Plato comes across as prolix, idealistic and almost mystical, while Aristotle is relentlessly practical and systematic. These generalisations are misleading, but there is some degree of truth in them. Plato is capable of passages like this:

....[W]e shall pass safely over the river of Forgetfulness and our soul will not be defiled. Wherefore my counsel is that we hold fast ever to the heavenly way and follow after justice and virtue always, considering that the soul is immortal and able to endure every sort of good and every sort of evil. Thus shall we live dear to one another and to the gods, both while remaining here and when, like conquerors in the games who go round to gather gifts, we receive our reward. And it shall be well with us both in this life and in the pilgrimage of a thousand years which we have been describing. (*Republic*, 621b-d; trans. Benjamin Jowett)

Whereas Aristotle is more like this:

> That moral virtue lies in the middle, then, and in what sense it does so, and that it lies in the middle between two vices, the one involving excess, the other deficiency, and that it does so because its character is to aim at what is intermediate in passions and in actions, has been sufficiently stated. Hence also it is no easy task to be good. For in everything it is no easy task to find the middle.... Anyone can get angry – that is easy – or give or spend money; but to do this to the right person, to the right extent, at the right time, with the right motive, and in the right way, that is not for everyone, nor is it easy; wherefore goodness is rare and laudable and noble. (*Nicomachean Ethics*, 1109a; trans. W.D. Ross (adapted))

Aristotle was as dry and pedantic as he was brilliant. To be fair, some of the dryness is no doubt due to the fact that his surviving works appear to take the form of lecture notes. His writings aren't as daunting as they may seem. The above passage, for example, is getting at the essentially simple point that virtue lies in the middle space between opposites – so, for example, courage lies in the middle between rashness and cowardice. The passage comes from Aristotle's great treatise on morality, the *Nicomachean Ethics*. This work was enormously influential in later times: fans included the Islamic philosopher Averroes and the Catholic theologian St Thomas Aquinas. It continues to be widely read and studied today. In it, Aristotle outlines his theories on the structure of the human soul, the theory and practice of virtue, the nature of friendship and pleasure, and various other matters.

For Aristotle, what is good (*agathon*) is what leads to a thing's "end" or "purpose" (*telos*). The ultimate *telos* of human affairs is *eudaimonia*. This word is generally translated as "happiness", but it has a slightly broader and fuller meaning in the Greek – Aristotle describes it as what renders life desirable and complete. Aristotle did not believe that happiness lay primarily in a person's external circumstances – he compared this view to attributing a skilled lyre-player's abilities to his owning a top-of-the-range lyre. Rather, he thought that the summit of *eudaimonia* was intellectual contemplation – a natural conclusion, perhaps, for a philosopher to reach.

Living virtuously was an integral part of *eudaimonia*, and Aristotle considered a whole catalogue of virtues in exhaustive detail. Other writers, including Plato and Cicero, wrote of four basic virtues – prudence, courage, temperance and justice. These became known as the "cardinal virtues". When put together with the three biblical virtues of faith, hope and charity, they were absorbed into the later Christian tradition as the seven "capital virtues".

You can see that the ancient philosophers had a liking for what is today known as "virtue ethics". This is one of the three main approaches to ethics in the Western tradition, the other two being consequentialism and deontology. Consequentialism teaches that the morality of an action is to be judged by its consequences – so, for example, it is an ethical act to torture a terrorist if it means that he will tell you where he's hidden the bomb. Deontology, by contrast, claims that the morality of an action is to be judged according to whether the action is good or bad in itself – so, for example, we can't torture the terrorist because torture is always inherently wrong. Virtue ethics provides an alternative approach to moral thinking. The important thing is not to construct an abstract principle which will enable us to figure out the "right" answer to moral dilemmas, as if ethical living was some kind of metaphysical maths test – it is to cultivate personal virtues which will lead us to act well in concrete situations. No wonder the likes of Aristotle went down so well in English public schools. The most accessible introduction to ancient virtue ethics for the modern layperson is probably Cicero's *On Duties* (*De Officiis*), which was the second book to be printed by Johannes Gutenberg after the Bible.

The ancient philosophers didn't concern themselves only with individual behaviour: they wrote about communal living too. Aristotle, for example, held that the city-state – the *polis* – was the summit of social organisation. He conceived it as a self-sufficient community whose *telos* was the good life of its inhabitants. He drew a distinction between good forms of government, which serve the common good, and bad forms, which serve the sectional interests of the rulers. His three "good" forms of government were monarchy, aristocracy and "polity" (*politeia*); these corresponded with rule by one man, by a group of men and by a broader spread of citizens. The three equivalent "bad" forms were tyranny, oligarchy and democracy. This highlights the fact that "democracy" was not a good word until very, very recently in European history: prior to the 20th century, it had connotations not of freedom and justice but of mob-rule and anarchy. Interestingly, Aristotle prefigured Karl Marx in discerning an underlying economic basis to the different forms of government: oligarchy was the self-interested rule of the rich, while democracy was the self-interested rule of the poor. Aristotle's favoured form of government was "polity" – a mixture of rule by the many and rule by the few, governed under the rule of law, in which the middle classes held the balance of power. Some might say that this is not dissimilar from the type of set-up that we have today.

Not that there aren't great differences between ancient and modern political attitudes, of course. Ancient political thought – like ancient society generally – tended to be prescriptive and communitarian rather than liberal and individualistic. Plato, for example, placed a premium on social harmony and the common good. Indeed, Plato took these ideas a bit too far, and he has gained something of a reputation as an enemy of freedom. It is fairly clear that he was opposed to Athenian democracy. In his masterpiece, the *Republic*, he admiringly describes an imaginary authoritarian state with a rigid social hierarchy, state control of the family and religion, eugenics, censorship, and false propaganda to keep the masses in their place. But this isn't necessarily as bad as it looks. It would be wrong to assume that Plato was offering the fictional city in the *Republic* as a blueprint for real-life Greek society. And it should be remembered that it was Plato who, in a later and less authoritarian work called the *Laws*, was responsible for fashioning the West's first philosophical exposition of the idea of the rule of law.

Plato was not alone in placing communal interests over individualism. Aristotle was less inclined than Plato to flirt with totalitarianism, but he explicitly argued that the laws of the state should *require* people to be good, since most people could not be trusted to be good by themselves. A movement of intellectual radicals called the Sophists put forward something resembling a modern liberal model of the state, but it never caught on. Aristotle expressly rejected their theories, according to which (he said) "the law is a treaty and a mutual guarantee of citizens' rights, but it cannot make them good and just" (*Politics*, 1280b).

One idea that recurs repeatedly in the Western political tradition is the idea of the mixed or balanced constitution. This might take the form of balancing different social groups – the king on his throne, the church and nobility in the House of Lords, and the commoners in the House of Commons. Alternatively, it might take the form of separating out the different functions of government – the executive, the legislature and the judiciary. It should come as no surprise that we owe the idea of the mixed constitution to the Greeks and Romans. We have seen that Aristotle advocated a mixture of oligarchy and democracy; Plato likewise advocated a mixture of monarchy and democracy. The historian Polybius was the first to develop in detail the idea that the best constitution is a three-part mixture of monarchy, oligarchy and democracy – he associated this model with Sparta and (in particular) with the Roman Republic. Similar ideas are found in other thinkers, including Cicero and the Stoics.

Having mentioned the Stoics, we might take a closer look at what this highly influential philosophical school taught and believed. In modern parlance, being "stoic" might mean no more than putting up with a painful ingrowing toenail without complaining. In the ancient world, however, Stoicism was a highly developed theory of human life and its place in the universe.

The Stoics emphasised detachment in the face of the ups and downs of life. The truly wise man would live passively in accordance with nature. He would observe an attitude of indifference – *apatheia*, from where we get "apathy" – towards external, non-essential things like wealth and poverty. Stoics taught that the usual attributes of good and bad fortune were "matters of indifference". Some, such as wealth, health and high social status, were "preferable", while others, such as poverty, pain and disease, were clearly not. But they were all ultimately unimportant. The goal of the Stoic was to embrace this realisation, to begin to perceive the world correctly, and to bring his unruly emotions under control. The Stoic attitude of indifference even extended to life itself: Stoics were quite sanguine about suicide. If one chose to carry on living, the key to happiness was virtue, which meant living in accordance with reason.

In its emphasis on divorcing oneself from the emotional roller-coaster of worldly existence, the Stoic philosophy bore some resemblance to Buddhism. (Incidentally, the Greeks and the Romans knew about Buddhism – the Christian writer Clement of Alexandria reported that "there are some among the Indians who follow the teachings of Boutta, whom they honour as a god because of his exceptional holiness" (*Stromata*, 1.15)). The ascetic aspects of Stoicism also influenced Christian moral ideas. Perhaps less obviously, the Stoic belief that a person's feelings can be reprogrammed by restructuring his thoughts about the world anticipated modern Cognitive Behavioural Therapy. It is a striking fact that ancient philosophy often had as much to do with what we would recognise as psychotherapy as with the abstract intellectual pursuit of truth. The Stoic philosopher Epictetus even claimed that "the philosopher's school is a doctor's surgery" (*Discourses*, 3.23.30).

One of the best-known Stoic or Stoic-influenced personalities of antiquity was the Emperor Marcus Aurelius (121 – 180 AD). Marcus kept a private philosophical diary during his reign, and by a miracle this document has survived to be handed down to modern times. Known as the *Meditations*, it is one of the most remarkable pieces of writing that we have from the ancient world – the personal journal of a Roman Emperor. The *Meditations* have been likened to a Western version of the *Tao Te Ching*, the Taoist scripture, and they have become a favourite of other world leaders, including Frederick the Great of Prussia and President Bill Clinton. They were, incidentally, composed in Greek: as we have seen, Greek was the common language of educated and philosophical writing in the Roman Empire.

Marcus seems to have favoured a form of rational introspection, coupled with an appreciation of the fragility of life and a Stoic indifference to its vicissitudes. A few quotes from the *Meditations* will give some idea of their general flavour:

Be in harmony with the things which you have been fated to experience. Love the people whom you have been fated to be joined with, and do so truly. (6.39)

Near is your forgetfulness of everything, and near is everyone's forgetfulness of you. (7.21)

It is ridiculous not to flee from your own faults, which you can do, but to flee from those of other people, which you cannot do. (7.71)

I have often been amazed at how each man loves himself more than everyone else, but treats his own opinion of himself as less important than the opinion of others. (12.4)

The principal philosophical rivals of the Stoics were the Epicureans, who took their name from the Greek thinker Epicurus (341 – 270 BC). It is well known that Epicurus advocated the pursuit of pleasure. What is not so well known is that this didn't mean that he encouraged his followers to live lives of hedonism. Indeed, his principal Roman disciple, Lucretius, wrote a famous diatribe against sexual love. Instead, Epicurus emphasised inner peace, serenity, the absence of pain and what was termed *ataraxia*, "not-being-hassled" – again, this is philosophy as therapy. He coined the slogan *lathe biósas*, which roughly translates as "keep your head down"; not bad life advice, then and now. Lucretius also thought that the Epicurean could draw satisfaction from observing the sorry state of less enlightened people. He expressed this in a famous metaphor:

How sweet, when the great waters of the sea are churned by
winds,

to watch from dry land another man desperately struggling....

(*De Rerum Natura*, 2.1-2)

We originally met Lucretius in Chapter 1, where I noted
that he took the unusual (by modern standards) step of penning a
treatise on atomic physics in verse. In fact, this treatise – an epic
poem entitled *De Rerum Natura*, or *On the Nature of Things* – is
one of the highlights of classical literature. It was highly thought
of back in ancient times, not least by Virgil, who was strongly
influenced by it. To this day, readers of a rationalist bent find
much to admire in Lucretius' presentation of Epicurean scientific
materialism. It was not for nothing that Karl Marx gave him an
honourable mention in his PhD thesis. Strictly speaking,
Lucretius and Epicurus were not atheists: they accepted in
principle the existence of the gods. But they denied that the gods
had any role in human affairs. Everything that happens in this
world was (they said) to be explained purely through the medium
of physical matter, the basic form of which consisted of
microscopic particles or atoms – *atomoi*, "indivisible things".
Not until the 19th century, with the advent of subatomic physics,
did scientists move beyond this paradigm.

However much they disagreed about things, the Stoics and the Epicureans – and, for that matter, Plato and Aristotle – were united by one common feature. They all saw the world as being in some sense *comprehensible*. They believed that, with some mixture of careful observation and rational thought, human beings could draw certain deductions and make certain claims about human life, the world and the cosmos. There was, however, a philosophical movement that had no time for this sort of thing. Members of this movement specialised in knowing nothing, or even in rejecting the very possibility of knowledge. They described their opponents – all of them – as "Dogmatists"; and they described themselves as "Sceptics".

Sceptics came in two varieties. There were the "Academic" Sceptics, who traced their lineage back to Socrates, the original restless, awkward questioner. And there were the "Pyrrhonian" Sceptics, who were inspired by Pyrrho of Elis (c.360 – c.270 BC). The Pyrrhonians were perhaps the most radical Sceptics. They were not only sceptical about the answers to the great philosophical questions: they were sceptical about the business of being sceptical.

The leading Sceptic writer Sextus Empiricus, whose day job was practising medicine, explained where the Sceptics were coming from. A man would begin by embracing the doctrines of one or another philosophical school; but, on encountering equally strong arguments against that school's position, he would fall into *ataraxia*:

> He begins to philosophise, to pass judgement upon ideas and to grasp which are true and which are false.... Then he encounters arguments of equal weight on both sides; and, being unable to pass judgement upon them, he suspends judgement. When he suspends judgement, *ataraxia* in matters of opinion fortuitously follows.... To be sure, we do not consider the sceptic to be entirely undisturbed, but we say that he is disturbed by things which are inevitable: we acknowledge that he is sometimes cold and thirsty and suffers things of that nature. (*Outlines of Pyrrhonism*, 1.25-29)

Yet even such things as cold and thirst will not disturb the Sceptic as much as they disturb other people, since he will experience them in serenity, without making value judgements about them. Note once again the psychological importance ascribed to philosophy, and the way that Sextus holds up *ataraxia* as an objective. For the Sceptic, as for the Epicurean and the Stoic, the quest for knowledge was ultimately less important than the quest for a quiet life.

*

The learned debates of Epicurus, Plato and the rest probably had little to do with the beliefs and practices of ordinary Greeks and Romans – as little as, say, the theological niceties of St Thomas Aquinas had to do with peasant girls casting folk-spells to get St Catherine to find them a husband. This first began to dawn on modern scholars at the end of the 19th century. Beneath the metaphysics of the philosophers, the lofty Olympian gods of Homer and the marble pediments of the Parthenon, scholars such as Sir James Frazer and Jane Ellen Harrison claimed to have discovered a wild popular religion of fertility spirits, folk demons and human sacrifices. Our ancient ancestors were not, it seemed, as civilised and rational as we might like to think. They were just as primitive and superstitious as... well, as the native peoples who were being brought into our expanding colonial empire.

This sort of thing can be overdone. Frazer and his followers, like all pioneers, were a bit too eager to prove their case, and many of their theories have not stood the test of time. The Greeks and the Romans were not especially irrational or primitive. All societies have divisions between folk beliefs and intellectual philosophy, and the Greeks and Romans had a more highly developed tradition of the latter than most. It is also likely that various elements of the intellectual philosophical tradition filtered down to become part of the common wisdom of the ancient world, known to Everyman: "Epicureans don't think the gods listen to our prayers", "Sceptics doubt stuff", and so on. Nevertheless, it is as well to bear in mind that the detailed and complex ideas that we read in texts like the dialogues of Plato would have been quite remote from the great majority of the people who lived in classical antiquity – just as a future historian would be unwise to assume that most people living in the 21st century West had read their Nietzsche, their Bertrand Russell or their Jacques Derrida.

We can't really know what most ordinary Greeks and Romans believed, but we have a pretty good idea of what they *did*. Graeco-Roman religion was mainly a matter of following traditional cult practices rather than signing up to creeds – in the terminology, it was focused on orthopraxy rather than orthodoxy. What mattered most was outward conduct rather than inward faith. In this sense, classical paganism had a very different set of priorities from Christianity. If the great sin of Christian times was heresy, or wrongful belief, the great sin of paganism was impiety, or wrongful deeds and words. People generally didn't care precisely what you believed as long as you celebrated the right festivals and observed the correct taboos – although it is only fair to note that there was also a strain of thought which emphasised the inner, ethical disposition of the worshipper.

The principal act of classical religion was sacrifice (*thysia* in Greek, *sacrificium* in Latin). Scholars have identified sacrifice as forming part of a relationship of reciprocity between humans and the gods. This reciprocity is labelled with the Greek word *kharis*, "grace" or "favour". Humans gave gifts to the gods through sacrifice, and in return they asked the gods through prayer for what they needed. Sacrifices could be regular, recurring ceremonies or one-off events. They often involved the killing of animals, although other foodstuffs were also used. One widespread method of sacrifice – libation – involved pouring out liquids, usually wine. In addition, material objects were sometimes dedicated to the gods, such as weapons after victory in a battle. There were priests to officiate at public sacrificial ceremonies, but there was no separate priestly class like the Indian Brahmans or the Catholic priesthood.

People were relatively indifferent to the idea of an afterlife, at least by comparison with Christian cultures, although they do seem to have believed that the spirits of the dead had some kind of existence after death, perhaps in an Underworld. Graeco-Roman religion was focused more on *this* world, and on the nature and deeds of the gods and spirits who pervaded the landscape of the ancient Mediterranean. The Greeks, as we know, left behind them a vast corpus of mythology. It is sometimes said that the Romans, by contrast, had a religion of rituals without many myths to go with them, and that they took over what mythology they had from the Greeks (turning Zeus into Jupiter, Aphrodite into Venus, and so on). This is a bit of an exaggeration. The Romans didn't leave behind a mountain of indigenous myths like the Greeks did, but they did leave some, if you know where to look for them.

Of course, not everyone believed in the official religion. Take the views of Pliny the Elder (23 – 79 AD), a kind of ancient Richard Dawkins. Pliny had this to say about beliefs in souls and an afterlife:

After burial we have vain speculations about spirits, although everyone is the same after his last day as he was before his first, and there is no more sensation in the body or mind after death than there is before birth. Typical human vanity stretches itself forward into the future and lyingly claims that it still has life even in the very hour of death.... But what is the actual substance of the soul? What material is it made of? How does it think? How can it see, hear or touch?... And where is the location, and how great is the multitude, of the souls or ghosts of so many centuries past? These are the fictions of childish fantasy and of a mortality which is unwilling ever to die. (*Natural History*, 7.55)

Pliny was a bit of a grumpy old man, however, and his uncompromisingly anti-religious views were not typical of mainstream Roman opinion. Edward Gibbon famously wrote in his *Decline and Fall of the Roman Empire* that the various forms of Roman paganism "were all considered by the people as equally true; by the philosophers as equally false; and by the magistrate as equally useful". However, this rather smug aphorism probably tells us more about Gibbon's own Enlightenment anti-clericalism than it does about religious belief in the ancient world. This raises a wider point, which we have met already but bears reiterating. When we write history, we constantly have to make sure that we are not really writing about ourselves.

*

The best-known religious text of the Graeco-Roman world is the Bible. The New Testament was composed in Greek, and even the Old Testament, which was originally written in Hebrew, was widely read and studied in a Greek translation known as the Septuagint. Judaism and Christianity had their origins among the Semitic cultures of the Middle East, but they came to be fixed features of the religious landscape of the Roman Empire.

As far as Judaism is concerned, one fact which is not always appreciated is that there were simply *more* Jews around, by head of population, in the ancient world. It is sometimes said that there would be several hundred million Jews alive today if it had not been for the successive waves of persecution in the intervening centuries. In fact, antisemitism was already a reality in ancient times. One reason why the Jews were the object of disapproval is that they insisted on worshipping a single deity rather than participating in the traditional Graeco-Roman polytheistic cults. The early Christians, of course, adopted the same stance. In both cases, this came across as highly provocative because it meant rejecting a fundamental plank of Graeco-Roman society which was closely intertwined with the institutions of state. The Jews tended to get away with it more than the Christians did because they could appeal to their ancestral customs, and the Romans in particular were very big on ancestral customs. However, it could lead to difficulties.

The Jewish philosopher Philo wrote a short book entitled *The Embassy to Gaius*, which gives a remarkable account of a face-to-face meeting between a group of Jewish ambassadors and the mad Emperor Caligula (reigned 37 – 41 AD; his birth name was Gaius, hence the title of the book). Caligula, who was allegedly the model for King Joffrey in *Game of Thrones,* might not have been quite as much of a maniac as some of our sources claim. It is clear, however, that he had something wrong with him mentally. The audience got off to a bad start:

JEWS: *(Bowing down low)* Greetings, O august Emperor!
CALIGULA: You are haters of the gods.

It becomes clear that Caligula is not happy because the Jews are refusing to worship him as a god – which is what he thinks he is. This was unusual even by the standards of Roman emperors, who usually waited until they had died before becoming divine. The Jews protest that they have offered sacrifices to Jehovah on his behalf. That's not the same, he replies. They should be sacrificing to him personally. At this point, the Jews start to physically tremble. The tension is temporarily broken as Caligula decides to take them for a walk around his estate while he inspects some building work. Then a question occurs to him:

CALIGULA: Why do you refuse to eat pork?
JEWS: Different nations have different laws. There are many who do not eat lamb, which is the tenderest of all meats.
CALIGULA: They are quite right. Lamb is not nice.
(Adapted from *Embassy*, 44-45)

At length, Caligula concludes that his Jewish guests are pitiable rather than dangerous, and sends them away. It was a narrow escape. Some later mad despots were not so forgiving.

The Jews may have had unorthodox religious views, but they were *mostly* accepted by their fellow imperial subjects. The same could not be said for the members of the early Christian church. To most classical pagans, the early Christians were a radical, subversive sect from the East, the sort of nonsense that women and slaves got mixed up in. There were even disturbing rumours that they held rites in which they ate human flesh and drank blood. For a respectable Roman pagan to become a Christian would have been roughly equivalent to a respectable Englishman today joining a flying saucer cult.

The key Christian texts, however, are less exotic than this might suggest. The New Testament was (as we have noted) written in Greek, and much of its contents are an identifiable product of the Graeco-Roman world. Some of its books, like the Epistle to the Hebrews and the Second Epistle of Peter, are written in accomplished Greek and can comfortably take their place alongside other examples of 1st century AD Greek literature. Something similar can be said of the New Testament's cultural background. Of course, this background has a strong Jewish element, as one would expect; but in other ways it fits comfortably within the Graeco-Roman world. For example, in the first three gospels (Matthew, Mark and Luke), Jesus appears as Rabbi Jeshua – a figure from a Jewish cultural background who teaches in down-to-earth parables and short, pithy sayings: "If anyone slaps you on the right cheek, turn the other cheek to him too"; "He who humbles himself will be raised up, and he who raises himself up will be humbled". By contrast, the fourth gospel (John) draws on the ideas of the Greek intellectual tradition and emphasises the mystical, cosmic mission of Christ: "In the beginning was the Word, and the Word was with God and the Word was God....". The "Word" here is the *"Logos"*, a technical term from Greek philosophy. Greek philosophical influences can also be seen in the epistles of St Paul, an important later source of Christian doctrine.

There is a temptation to focus on the New Testament as the principal religious text produced by the Graeco-Roman world. But this is only because we know how the story went on from there. We know that Christianity became the dominant religion of the Roman Empire, and of the European states that succeeded it. At the time, however, there was nothing that would have seemed inevitable about this. The Mediterranean basin in the first few centuries AD was thick with religious traditions, ideas and sects of wildly different kinds, from old-style Graeco-Roman civic religion to the Egyptian cults of Isis and Serapis, and from the eunuch priests of Cybele to the mysterious Mithraic movement (a kind of ancient Freemasonry). The great Roman historian Keith Hopkins attempted to capture some of this religious ferment in his book *A World Full of Gods*.

Moving away from the familiar waters of Christianity and Judaism, it is worth casting an eye over some lesser-known religious movements and texts from the ancient world. Let us take, for example, the Hermetic Corpus. This is a series of religious and philosophical writings penned in Egypt between roughly the 1st and 3rd centuries AD, at a time when Egypt was culturally part-Greek and politically Roman. The texts are accordingly cosmopolitan in character. Scholars have argued over whether the ideas in the Corpus are mostly Greek or mostly Egyptian; they are probably both. When the works were rediscovered in the Renaissance, it was initially thought that they dated back to the earliest days of ancient Egypt, and so represented primaeval wisdom from the dawn of civilisation. This dating was subsequently refuted, but the ideas in them could still be very old.

The Hermetic Corpus affirms that behind mankind, the world and even the gods themselves stands a transcendent, ineffable, pantheistic divinity:

Holy art Thou, more powerful than all power.

Holy art Thou, transcending all pre-eminence.

Holy Thou art, Thou better than all praise.

Accept my reason's offerings pure, from soul and heart for aye stretched up to Thee, O Thou unutterable, unspeakable, Whose Name naught but the Silence can express. (1.31; trans. G.R.S.Mead)

The central claims of the Corpus are that man has both physical/mortal and spiritual/divine aspects; and that by attaining "knowledge" (*gnósis*) he can transcend his mortality and enter into divinity. In this context, "knowledge" is not knowledge of the intellectual kind that is handed out in schools and universities, but the kind of inner experience of the divine that mystics of all religions write about. Ancient religion wasn't all about sacrifices and festivals – it had a mystical strand which bears some resemblance to Eastern religions.

The Hermetic movement was not alone in espousing this kind of religiosity. There were other esoteric philosophical schools in the ancient world which drew on much the same ideas and acquired their own sacred writings and groups of followers. Prominent among these was Gnosticism. As the name suggests, Gnosticism placed great emphasis on *gnósis*, the "knowledge" thing. It influenced the early Christian church, but ended up being denounced as a heresy. Our understanding of Gnosticism took a great leap forward when a cache of Gnostic scriptures was discovered at Nag Hammadi in Egypt in 1945. This was an incredibly lucky find, and it cast a great deal of light on Gnostic beliefs. The Nag Hammadi texts are quite unlike both orthodox Christian texts and mainstream Greek philosophy. One text, for example, known as the "Gospel of the Egyptians", sounds vaguely like something out of Harry Potter:

And thus there came forth from above the power of the great light, the Manifestation. She gave birth to the four great lights: Harmozel, Oroiael, Davithe, Eleleth, and the great incorruptible Seth, the son of the incorruptible man Adamas.

And thus the perfect hebdomad, which exists in hidden mysteries, became complete. When she receives the glory, she becomes eleven ogdoads.

And the Father nodded approval; the whole pleroma of the lights was well pleased. Their consorts came forth for the completion of the ogdoad of the divine Autogenes.... (tr. Alexander Bohlig and Frederik Wisse)

The other major contemporary esoteric movement was Neoplatonism. As the name suggests, this was a philosophical school which drew its inspiration from the works of Plato. The Neoplatonists would have seen themselves simply as Platonists, following in the footsteps of the master; but their ideas were sufficiently distinct from Plato's to warrant being classified separately. They were highly erudite philosophers who produced complex and challenging works which are still read today – but they had a mystical streak as well. Like the Hermeticists and the Gnostics, they embraced ideas of communion with the ineffable divine. Some of them, like the Syrian writer Iamblichus, pioneered a form of practical magic or "theurgy" which was aimed at bringing about this communion: it seems to have involved mysterious ceremonies in which supernatural powers were invoked through sacrifices, rituals and sacred symbols. The Emperor Julian (reigned 361 – 363 AD) drew on Neoplatonic theology in a final attempt to reconstruct and reinvigorate classical paganism in the face of the advance of Christianity. But by then it was too late.

The exotic brew of mystical ideas deriving from Hermeticism, Gnosticism and Neoplatonism lingered on in the Western intellectual tradition. Their influence on mainstream Christian theology was rather limited, at least in Western Europe – Aristotle came to be much more important in this regard, thanks to his hugely influential admirer St Thomas Aquinas. But they became central to what we would today call esotericism or occultism.

6. Tragedy and Some Tragedians

Greek tragedy must follow hard on the heels of Greek philosophy as one of the best known legacies of the ancient world. In the last few decades, Greek tragedies have become more popular than they have been at any time since antiquity. They have proved to be a particularly popular way of exploring contemporary political and social problems. Euripides' *Trojan Women*, for example, has been appropriated by anti-war movements, while his *Bacchae* has been used to comment on drug addiction. Modern writers have produced their own adaptations of ancient tragedies. Jean Anouilh's *Antigone*, which was named after the tragedy of the same name by Sophocles, has had the rare honour of being interpreted both as a cry for individual freedom against the state and as an apologia for fascism.

Tragedy appears to have had its origins in religious ritual of some sort. The word means literally "goat-song", *tragóidia*, a strange term whose meaning is still obscure. Perhaps surprisingly, ancient tragedies didn't need to be "tragic" in the modern sense of the word. There are examples of tragedies with happy endings. Generally speaking, however, tragic drama involved death, war, family feuds, incest, cannibalism and other such things, so the semantic difference is not all that important.

When we speak of ancient tragedy or Greek tragedy, we essentially mean *Athenian* tragedy, since it was at Athens that the art form came into its own. In classical times, tragic plays were performed there during the Great Dionysia, an annual festival held in honour of the god Dionysus. What this performance context means for the interpretation of the plays has been the subject of debate among scholars. Depending on who you listen to, the fact that the plays were performed among the various civic and religious rituals of the Dionysia is either a key part of understanding what they mean or else an irrelevant coincidence.

Tragedies were performed at the Dionysia in trilogies (from the Greek *trilogia*, "three works"). The three plays of a trilogy could, but did not have to, deal with successive stages of the same story. A trilogy was generally followed by a shorter, lighter work known as a satyr play. Three different playwrights competed at the Dionysia each year. Of the three greatest Athenian tragic playwrights, Aeschylus (c.525 – c.455 BC) is said to have won the contest 13 times, Sophocles (c.495 – c.405 BC) 18 times and Euripides (c.480 – c.406 BC) five times.

Greek tragedies tended to be structurally similar – between 1,000 and 2,000 lines long, and limited in their focus to one day

153

and one location. They could, however, include several different literary and dramatic styles – set-piece speeches by characters; odes sung by a Chorus; an *agón*, or debate; and *stichomythia*, or rapid one-line dialogue. The interplay of spoken and sung text is vaguely reminiscent of modern opera – and indeed, opera was invented in Renaissance Italy by dramatists who were attempting to recreate ancient tragic drama.

The vast majority of Athenian tragedies have been lost, and the only complete tragic trilogy which survives is Aeschylus' *Orestes Plays*, or *Oresteia*. Aside from the *Oresteia*, only four other plays by Aeschylus survive out of a total original corpus of between 70 and 90. This rate of loss is not unusual for an ancient author, although that doesn't make it any less lamentable. The *Oresteia* is the first of several ancient tragedies which I want to look at in this chapter. It is one of the seminal literary works of Western culture – up there with the Homeric epics and *War and Peace*, as well as the many works that were directly or indirectly influenced by it, from Shakespeare's *Hamlet* to Wagner's *Ring of the Nibelung*. It was probably Aeschylus' last production at Athens, and it premiered at the Great Dionysia in 458 BC. Predictably, it won first prize.

The *Oresteia* deals with the story of Agamemnon, Clytaemnestra and Orestes. We have already encountered this legendary tale as a recurring theme in the *Odyssey*. Agamemnon returns home from the Trojan War; he is killed by Aegisthus, the lover of his wife Clytaemnestra; and his murder is avenged by his son Orestes. Homer uses the story as a counterpoint to the main plot, Odysseus' triumphant return home to his faithful wife and son. In Aeschylus, however, the story is the main focus of the action.

The events of the *Oresteia* form the climactic episode in a longer mythological saga involving a terrible ancestral curse which lies on Agamemnon's family, the royal house of Argos (also known as the "Pelopids"). According to the mythology, the troubles went back to the founders of the dynasty, Tantalus and his son Pelops. Things really got going, however, when Pelops had two sons of his own, Atreus and Thyestes. Thyestes seduced Atreus' wife and attempted to usurp his throne. Atreus duly drove Thyestes out into exile. He then pretended to forgive him, secretly killed his sons, and served them up to him at a banquet. If this was not enough, Thyestes raped his daughter Pelopeia, and she duly gave birth to Aegisthus.

The curse worked its way down to the next generation as Agamemnon, the son of Atreus, was preparing to embark on the military expedition that would become the Trojan War. Agamemnon mustered the Greek forces at Aulis in central

Greece; but, on attempting to sail onwards to Troy, he was confronted with strong adverse winds sent by the goddess Artemis. The army was stranded and began to starve. Artemis would allow the men to continue onwards to Troy only if Agamemnon sacrificed his daughter, Iphigeneia, to her. Agamemnon could either disband the army and call off the expedition – or he could kill his child.

Calling off the campaign to take back Helen because of adverse weather conditions would have been a humiliating climb-down, but that didn't mean that Agamemnon had to kill Iphigeneia. Nevertheless, he persuaded himself that he was justified in taking this course. Agamemnon had an unenviable choice, but it was a choice nonetheless. As Aeschylus puts it in a memorable and enigmatic phrase, *"anankas edu lepadnon"* – "he put on the harness of necessity". The family curse presented him with his dilemma, but he took upon himself the responsibility and guilt of resolving it by sacrificing his daughter. (Please note that this is just my interpretation of the story. Others would frame the issue differently and argue that Agamemnon had no true choice at all – the great classicist Sir Denys Page even made up a fictional interview with Aeschylus in which he put that interpretation into the tragedian's mouth. Read the plays and decide for yourself.)

The first play of the *Oresteia*, entitled *Agamemnon*, recounts Agamemnon's return to Argos and his murder at the hand of Clytaemnestra. The *Agamemnon* is a *tour de force*, even two and a half millennia after it was written. It is the most tragic of tragedies. There is a pervasive darkness in the play, punctuated by anguish. It opens with an ominous speech by a watchman who has been detailed to keep an eye out for the fire signal which will (it is hoped) announce the fall of Troy. It becomes clear that something is very wrong in the royal household – and it has something to do with the queen, a "woman whose heart plots like a man".

Clytaemnestra duly appears. She is hard-headed and proud; deceitful and duplicitous in her speech; and murderously violent in her actions. She kills Agamemnon alone and unaided, without Aegisthus even being present in the palace at the time. For an audience of Athenian men, brought up to expect women to be veiled, secluded and obedient, Clytaemnestra must have presented a harrowing spectacle.

Aeschylus was preoccupied with the role of the gods in human affairs. Zeus is presented as a mysterious supreme deity; he is spoken of as a god of justice, but it is a harsh, primitive justice based on violence and revenge. It was Zeus, as the god of guests, who caused the ten years of slaughter of the Trojan War in

157

retribution for Paris's violation of the laws of hospitality. One of those who got killed in the process was Iphigeneia – and it looks like Agamemnon will be next, and then Clytaemnestra... and so on, in endless succession. Crime breeds crime and murder breeds murder. If there is any hope, it is only through learning this hard lesson. Zeus, we are told, has laid down the law of *"pathei mathos"*, "learning through suffering". Men must become wise against their will. It was these lines, incidentally, that Bobby Kennedy famously quoted to a tense audience of black Americans after Martin Luther King's assassination; they were later carved on his tombstone.

When Agamemnon arrives on stage, he is careful to pay tribute piously to the gods – but it is far too late for that now. He initially refuses to enter the palace by stepping on a valuable fabric which Clytaemnestra has spread before him. Such an honour, as he says, is for a god and not a man. But his scruples quickly pass: he steps on the fabric and enters the palace, never to be seen alive again. It is the last bad decision he ever makes.

Agamemnon has brought with him the Trojan princess Cassandra as a slave and concubine. Cassandra has the gift of being able to prophecy with complete accuracy – but at the price of no-one believing what she says. She is the only one who sees clearly what a terrible predicament she, Agamemnon and the household are in. In a scene that would test any actress to the limit, she erupts into a half-mad prophetic frenzy. She tells the assembled Chorus of senior citizens what she sees with her second sight:

> A house which hates the gods – which knows death upon
> death of kinsfolk – and severed heads –
> which murders men – and where the floors run with blood!
> (1090-1092)

But, of course, no-one realises what she is getting at, even when she speaks entirely unambiguously:

> CASSANDRA: I tell you, you will see Agamemnon dead!
> CHORUS: Hush, poor woman, put your mouth to rest.
> (1246-1247)

When the deed is done, Clytaemnestra herself attributes the killing to the family's "revenge-spirit". It is not that she shirks taking responsibility for her crime – on the contrary, she proudly declares it to be a just revenge for the death of Iphigeneia (this is slightly undercut by the fact that she has also killed Cassandra, an innocent girl). But at the same time she realises that she is the agent of an ancestral curse. She tells the Chorus:

> Now your mouth is speaking the truth,
> naming this family's
> spirit, thrice fattened on blood;
> it nourishes terrible blood-licking
> lust; before the old wound
> is healed, a new one suppurates. (1475-1480)

Oddly enough, she does not arrive at the logical conclusion that she is next for an early grave. Even the dimwitted Chorus realise *that* much. With an altogether uncharacteristic naivety, she expresses a hope that the bloodshed is all over and that everything will be ok from now on.

It isn't. Clytaemnestra's son and nemesis Orestes appears in the next part of the trilogy, *The Libation-Bearers*. This is another play of darkness and vengeful anguish. The work is named for its Chorus, which is composed of women who are bearing libations to the grave of Agamemnon. The characters' overall frame of reference is still that of primitive rough justice which manifests itself as violent revenge, overseen by the majesty of Zeus. The Chorus sings:

Indeed it is the law that drops of murdered
blood flowing to the ground call forth more
blood; for slaughter cries for a Fury
from those who now have perished, bringing
further disaster upon disaster. (400-404)

This time, however, it is the Chorus which mistakenly thinks that the curse is about to be lifted.

Orestes is reunited with his sister Electra, and sets about taking revenge on his mother and her consort. Aegisthus is the first to die. Clytaemnestra poses more of a problem. Daunted by the prospect of matricide, Orestes hesitates before killing her. But he has been ordered by Apollo to avenge Agamemnon's death. We are told that Apollo has promised to protect Orestes if he sees the deed through, but has threatened him with chastisement by his father's avenging spirits, or Furies, if he doesn't. But what about *Clytaemnestra's* Furies? It looks like Orestes is damned if he does and damned if he doesn't. He has an even harder choice to make than his father.

He decides to kill his mother. This turns out to be the right decision, but it takes some time for this to become clear. At the end of *The Libation-Bearers*, Clytaemnestra's Furies appear and drive Orestes from the stage. He flees to take refuge in Apollo's great temple at Delphi, and it is there that we find him at the beginning of the third play, *The Kindly Ones*, which is named for its Chorus of Furies: "Kindly Ones" was a euphemistic term for these fearsome goddesses.

Apollo appears and tells Orestes to go to Athens, where he will help him put his case to a criminal court presided over by the goddess Athena. This is the point around which the trilogy turns. From now on, guilt and punishment will be matters for judicial process, not private revenge. In the *Agamemnon*, legal terms are used as metaphors for lawless violence; no-one seriously expects Clytaemnestra and Agamemnon to fight it out in court. The notion of judicial punishment is likewise mentioned in *The Libation Bearers*, but it is dismissed with a reaffirmation of the rightness of blood-vengeance:

> CHORUS: Pray for some god or mortal to come against them [Clytaemnestra and Aegisthus].
> ELECTRA: Do you mean a judge or an avenger?
> CHORUS: Say simply someone who will kill the killers.
> ELECTRA: Is it pious for me to ask this of the gods?
> CHORUS: How is it not, to give enemies ill for ill?
> (119-123)

Now there is going to be a real trial with real judges – selected citizens of Athens, presided over by Athena. In order to try Orestes, Athena decides to establish the Areopagus, a real-life Athenian homicide court. The use of this institution as the trial venue may have been Aeschylus' own invention. The Areopagus was an aristocratic body, and shortly before the *Oresteia*'s premiere it had seen its constitutional powers reduced to purely judicial functions as part of the entrenchment of Athenian democracy. It is not clear whether Aeschylus was supporting this development (by emphasising the body's judicial role) or opposing it (by presenting the body as a venerable, god-endorsed institution).

The Furies are the embodiment of the conception of justice as revenge which has driven the action of the trilogy up to this point. Their case is that Orestes has committed the unforgivable sin of killing his mother, a blood relative. Clytaemnestra's crime, by contrast, was to kill a man who was not related to her by blood. In his address to the court, Apollo attacks this case on the grounds that children are begotten solely by their fathers, with the mother playing the role of an incubator for the embryo. We know from other sources that this claim was in line with ancient Greek medical theories.

When the judges vote, the numbers turn out to be equal on each side. Athena delivers her casting vote for Orestes. She has no mother, being born from the head of Zeus, and so she is "strongly on the side of the father" (*"karta tou patros"*). She will not, therefore, consider the matricide of Clytaemnestra to be uniquely heinous, particularly as Clytaemnestra herself was guilty of killing her husband. The Furies protest that a younger generation of gods is usurping their ancient prerogatives, and Athena compensates them by giving them an honoured sanctuary in her city.

The trilogy has a "happy" ending insofar as it sees the family curse broken and the bloodfeud resolved through legal process, thanks to the institutions of the Athenian state. The darkness lifts – but only at the very end of the last play. The eventual resolution is purchased only after a long time and at a heavy cost, with a great capacity for human stupidity and violence being revealed in the process. Learning through suffering, indeed.

*

So much for Aeschylus. Let's now move on to consider what the other great Athenian tragedians, Euripides and Sophocles, made of the story. Both playwrights wrote plays called *Electra* which, like *The Libation-Bearers*, dealt with the circumstances surrounding Orestes' killing of Clytaemnestra. Electra, as you may remember, is Orestes' sister; she sent him abroad for safety when he was a small child.

To start with Euripides' *Electra* – Euripides' version of the story doesn't have the dark grandeur of Aeschylus', and the emphasis is different. The ancestral curse of the royal family is mentioned; and it is explained at the end of the play that the curse, along with the powers of fate and necessity, have been working away behind the action. But these large, menacing themes aren't pervasive in the same way that they are in the *Oresteia*. Euripides also gets in a direct dig at Aeschylus. The older man's Electra had recognised her brother by a lock of his hair, the appearance of his footprints and some of the clothes she wove for him. Euripides' Electra points out that comparing hair and footprints are feeble ways for a sister to identify a brother, and asks why a grown man would still have his baby clothes.

Euripides has something of a reputation as a subversive thinker. In the McCarthy era, he was famously cited by Congressman Joe Starnes of Alabama as an ancient Greek example of a Communist. And indeed he works a few lines into the *Electra* which challenge traditional social hierarchies –

although this would not have been an altogether subversive sentiment in democratic Athens. In other plays, he challenges traditional Athenian ideas about gender roles, but he is less interested in doing this in the *Electra*. Indeed, he has Electra remind us that men were supposed to wear the trousers in Athenian society, and also that women and children were supposed to be identified by reference to their menfolk:

> All among the Argives you would hear this said:
> "That woman's husband" – never "that man's wife".
> It is a disgrace for the woman to rule
> the house, and not the man; and I hate it when
> children are publicly called not after
> their father, the male, but after their mother. (930-935)

We are shown Electra lamenting vehemently for her murdered father Agamemnon, and wishing that Clytaemnestra could be killed. Aegisthus has attempted to take her out of the picture by marrying her off to an anonymous peasant. The peasant, knowing his place, has not attempted to consummate the union, something for which Electra is grateful. The play contains an interesting debate or *agón* between Electra and Clytaemnestra about the right and wrongs of how things have worked out. When

Clytaemnestra finally appears on stage, it turns out that she is a less formidable character than her Aeschylean incarnation – a somewhat haunted figure who is troubled by what she has done. She tells the story of Iphigeneia, adding the new twist that she was prepared to let the killing of her daughter go – it was Agamemnon's crassly insensitive decision to bring Cassandra home as a concubine that was the last straw. And if men could have mistresses, why shouldn't she shack up with Aegisthus?

It might be thought that this is just good old Euripides being subversive and presenting a sympathetic version of Clytaemnestra. But he also puts some telling counter-arguments into Electra's mouth. In particular, Electra deploys the crucial argument, which is very difficult to answer from within Clytaemnestra's frame of reference: if revenge, tit-for-tat, is a cogent moral principle, Clytaemnestra has no grounds for complaining if Orestes and Electra now kill her. She should have thought through the consequences before she chose to kill her husband: her regret, such as it is, has come too late.

When Orestes arrives, he kills Aegisthus without much difficulty. The killing takes place off-stage, and a messenger recounts that he accepted hospitality from Aegisthus prior to killing him, a rather troubling breach of Greek values (Electra's peasant husband, by contrast, virtuously welcomes Orestes and his companion into his humble home). As in the *Oresteia*, Orestes hesitates before killing his mother, but he and Electra nevertheless proceed to murder her, an act which they quickly come to regret.

The play is brought to an end by means of an ancient dramatic device known as a *Deus ex machina* – the sudden arrival of a god, or in this case gods, from a crane suspended above the set. (This is the origin of the modern sense of the phrase *Deus ex machina* – someone or something which appears suddenly to change or resolve a situation.) The gods are Clytaemnestra's brothers, Castor and Polydeuces. They acknowledge that Clytaemnestra's killing was just, but they tell Orestes that he was not entitled to carry it out. He will now need to go to Athens and stand trial at the Areopagus: he will be acquitted and will then live out his days in comfortable exile. The divinities add the surprising detail that Apollo himself (also known as Phoebus) acted wrongly in telling him to kill his mother:

> Her fate is just, but your deed was not just:
> Phoebus, Phoebus – he is my Lord, so I say
> no more. He is wise; his oracle was not wise.
> (1244-1246)

They also say that Helen never really went to Troy. It was a phantom that went there – a trick played by Zeus in order to provoke the slaughter of the Trojan War (this idea was not Euripides' – it went back to the archaic poet Stesichorus). The Greek gods, being anthropomorphic, could always be represented as having human weaknesses, but Euripides' gods are perhaps unusually fallible and capricious. His portrayal of the divine certainly lacks the majesty of Aeschylus'. It is arguably in this respect that the play is most "subversive".

*

The final surviving classical Greek treatment of the story comes to us from Sophocles in the form of his *Electra*. At least, most scholars believe that Sophocles' play is later than Euripides' – there is disagreement on this point, and we can't really resolve the question at this distance. Like Euripides' play, Sophocles' lacks the austere grandeur of the *Oresteia*. Its frame is domestic rather than cosmic. Again, the ancestral curse is referred to but not emphasised.

The most striking feature of the play is the character of Electra. Sophocles' heroine is a more extreme version of

Euripides' – a half-maddened figure stricken with misery and unrestrained lamentation:

> No, never will
>
> I stop my dirges and hateful groaning
>
> while I look on the shining,
>
> twinkling stars and this light of day....
>
> O House of Hades and Persephone [Queen of the
> Underworld],
>
> O Hermes of the Earth and Lady Curse,
>
> and Furies, fearsome daughters of the gods...
>
> come, help me, avenge my
>
> father's murder,
>
> and send me my brother:
>
> for I can no longer bear the crushing
>
> burden of my grief. (103-120)

She is given a sister, Chrysothemis, as a foil. It becomes clear that Chrysothemis has decided to collaborate with Clytaemnestra and Aegisthus' regime. The two sisters engage in *agónes*: Electra represents the qualities of courageous but hopeless moral absolutism and Chrysothemis those of level-headed pragmatism in the face of impossible odds. There is nothing like this clash of worldviews in Euripides' play. When she hears a false report that Orestes has died, Electra falls into despair and asks Chrysothemis to join her as she takes the extraordinary step of carrying out the killings herself (this proves to be unnecessary, as Orestes soon reveals himself).

Some years ago, when I was a postgraduate student, I wrote an article about the role that gender plays in Sophocles' *Electra*. Both Clytaemnestra and Electra represent problems from the point of view of Athenian ideas about gender. Neither woman is playing out the role laid down for her. It is made clear that Electra is unmarried, without even a nominal husband, and it is arguable that her semi-deranged lamentations are a symptom of her condition – it was believed that prolonged virginity was unhealthy for a woman, and that it led to madness. This was part of a bundle of strange theories that Greek doctors had about "women's problems": it is no coincidence, for example, that the term "hysteria" comes from the Greek word *hystér*, "uterus". On the other hand, it is easy to get carried away with this stuff. Chrysothemis is a virgin too, and she seems perfectly sane. Similarly, some post-Freudian psychiatrists speak of an "Electra complex", the female counterpart to the Oedipus complex, and it could be argued that there is an incestuous dimension to Electra's attachment to Agamemnon. This interpretation influenced

171

Richard Strauss' rendition of the story in his 1909 opera *Elektra*. On the whole, however, it is probably misleading and anachronistic to interpret Sophocles' play in these terms.

Sophocles' Clytaemnestra, like her counterpart in Euripides, is a less menacing figure than the Clytaemnestra of the *Oresteia*. She shows some maternal affection when she is told that Orestes has died. Electra engages in an *agón* with her, and Clytaemnestra brings up Iphigeneia's murder in defence of her actions. Electra duly makes the point that the principle of death for death would condemn Clytaemnestra too. More interestingly, however, Electra adds the new detail that Agamemnon *had* to sacrifice Iphigeneia because Artemis would not even let the Greeks return *home* from Aulis: she wasn't just blocking their way onwards to Troy. The army was trapped and destined to waste away. It was one person's life against thousands. If Agamemnon had no real choice in the matter, does that mean that Clytaemnestra's deed was therefore less justifiable and that the killing of Clytaemnestra herself is in turn less morally dubious?

Certainly, Orestes shows no hesitation in killing either Aegisthus or his mother, and it is a striking feature of the play that no overt sign is given that Orestes is doing anything wrong in any of this. There are no Furies; there is no hint of a trial. At the most, the text gives us a few clues that could be interpreted as meaning that the suffering is not yet over, such as the following exchange between Orestes and Aegisthus:

> ORESTES: Go inside, and quickly; for it is not words
> that are at issue any longer, but your life.
> AEGISTHUS: Why do you take me inside? If this deed is good,
> why must you have darkness – why not kill me here?
> ORESTES: Give me no orders. Go to the place where
> you killed my father: that is where you will die.
> AEGISTHUS: Ah! Must this house see, must it see the woes
> of the sons of Pelops now and in the future?
> ORESTES: It will see yours – in that, I am a sure prophet.
> AEGISTHUS: Your father could not claim such prophetic gifts.
> (1491-1500)

Yet the potentially ominous hints in this exchange don't really go anywhere. The play ends with an unambiguous song of triumph from the Chorus.

Sophocles' unfortunate refusal to tell us what to think has resulted in a long-running debate over whether or not Orestes has done the right thing. This gives something of a contrast with the earlier plays. The *Oresteia* makes it clear that the matricide was, at the least, a morally problematic act: Orestes needed to stand trial in a court of law and only narrowly escaped the Furies.

Euripides has his *Dei ex machina* say explicitly that Orestes should not have carried out the killing. Sophocles' *Electra*, however, leaves the moral judgement up to us.

*

Finally in this chapter, we will briefly consider a Roman take on the story.

Tragedy may have been largely an Athenian thing, but some Roman writers composed tragedies too – even Ovid, the counter-cultural love poet. Most of our surviving Latin tragedies were written by Seneca the Younger (c.1 BC – 65 AD), a writer and Stoic philosopher from Roman Spain. Seneca was an interesting character. He managed to fall out with two consecutive emperors, Caligula and Claudius, but bounced back to secure a position as tutor to their successor, the deranged egomaniac Nero. He managed to amass considerable wealth and power, and he lived to a ripe old age (by Roman standards) before Nero too got fed up with him and ordered him to commit suicide.

History has not always been kind to Seneca. From ancient times, writers have pointed to the incongruity of a Stoic philosopher living among enormous wealth and working for a tyrant like Nero. His writings, however, deserve to be taken on their own merits. They reveal a man who was both a competent literary stylist and a competent philosopher, although it is still debated just how original he was. Whatever one thinks of his personal behaviour, his works are still accessible and rewarding to the modern reader. Indeed, they are perhaps the best introductions to Stoic philosophy that have survived. I would particularly recommend the Oxford World's Classics translations.

As for Seneca's dramatic works, there survive ten tragedies which are attributed to him, eight of which are believed to be genuine. Through these plays, Seneca ended up strongly influencing the English dramatic tradition, not least through his influence on William Shakespeare. Perhaps ironically, it still remains unclear whether Seneca's works were intended for actual performance on stage. At any event, he wrote his own version of the *Agamemnon*, together with a prequel called *Thyestes* in which the eponymous character is shown gorged with the flesh of his own sons. Seneca didn't really do subtlety – T.S.Eliot once said that his characters "all seem to speak with the same voice, and at the top of it" (*Essays on Elizabethan Drama* (New York: Harcourt, Brace & World, 1960), 4).

With Seneca, we are back in a vaguely Aeschylean world of darkness and horror, and indeed his *Agamemnon* is clearly influenced by the *Oresteia*. In spite of the play's title,

Agamemnon himself is hardly a presence in the drama at all; he is given only 26 lines out of 1,012. The role of the ancestral curse is brought out from the beginning, as the play begins with an appearance from Thyestes' ghost:

> Leaving the dark realms of infernal Hades,
> I come, sent forth from Tartarus' deep pit,
> uncertain which place I hate the more: I, Thyestes,
> flee the infernal realms and scare away the world above....
> (1-4)

Thyestes' ghost, incidentally, is a lineal ancestor of the ghost of Hamlet's father which appears at the start of Shakespeare's *Hamlet*.

Clytaemnestra later returns to the theme of the history of the house of Pelops and the unending sequence of crime and revenge, as she refers to the sacrifice of Iphigeneia:

> O dynasty! Always crowning crimes with crimes:
> we bought fair winds with blood and war with a murder!
> (169-170)

As we might expect, Seneca's Clytaemnestra is a fearsome character, somewhat like Aeschylus'. She has already told herself:

....The better path is now closed off.
Once, you could have kept your marital bed pure
and kept your widowed sceptre with chaste faith.
Morals, justice, honour, piety and faith are dead,
and shame, which cannot return once it has gone.
Give the reins to all depravity, spur it onwards:
the safest way for crime lies always through crime.
(109-115)

Yet she is also an emotional woman. She hesitates to kill Agamemnon, but she is urged on in the plan by Aegisthus. Gender is an issue in the play. For example, this exchange takes place immediately after Agamemnon has been killed:

CLYTAEMNESTRA: Enemy of your mother, insolent and bold one,
by what right do you, a virgin, show yourself in public?
ELECTRA: As a virgin, I have fled from a house of adultery....
CLYTAEMNESTRA: You have a swollen heart and a man's spirit;
but, tamed by suffering, you will learn a woman's part.

ELECTRA: Unless my eyes deceive me, the sword is a woman's part.
(953-960)

The two women pose a clear challenge to proper gender roles. The characters accuse each other in turn of acting improperly, even to the extent of taking up arms – and each has a valid point. But the gender issues are not explored in depth: that was not Seneca's main concern.

We see Electra sending the infant Orestes away. We know that he is eventually going to return and kill Clytaemnestra, and that he will accordingly be afflicted by her Furies, because Cassandra tells us so. But there is otherwise little hint in the play of what is going to follow. It is a largely self-contained drama.

Seneca gives us some lines about the power and oppression of kings, and Aegisthus is depicted as something of a stereotypical tyrant (just as the character Atreus was in *Thyestes*). Given that Seneca worked for the Emperor Nero, it is tempting to surmise that he had his boss in mind when writing this stuff – but that may be a little too glib. More convincingly, we may find in the play clear evidence of Seneca's Stoic convictions, including the fickleness of fortune, the importance of detachment from the vicissitudes of life, and the desirability of suicide – all presented in carefully crafted, rhetorical language. For all its echoes of

Aeschylus, Seneca's *Agamemnon* is in this respect a world away from the high days of Athenian tragedy. It is a work composed not by a populist playwright hoping to win a festival prize, but by a court politician toying with philosophy and rhetoric in his lamplit study in Rome.

7. Oratory and the Orator

The orator is one of the stereotypical images of Roman culture: a toga-wearing statesman rousing the masses in the Forum with an impassioned speech in favour of war with Carthage or a cancellation of debts. The dramatic turning point of Shakespeare's *Julius Caesar* is a famous piece of oratory put into the mouth of Mark Antony, Caesar's loyal lieutenant, as he incites the Roman people against the assassins of the dead dictator – "Friends, Romans, countrymen....". The tradition of classical rhetoric persisted in European culture for centuries. Together with grammar and logic, it was one of the *trivium* of subjects that were taught in universities into the Middle Ages. Oratorical talent was an important part of political success well into the age of modern mass media, as the names Mussolini, Hitler and Churchill bear witness. To some extent, it still is today.

Long before the Romans came along, rhetoric had been a live issue in the small *poleis* of classical Greece. Skill at winning round one's fellow citizens by talking at them persuasively could be the key to success in the law courts, the assembly and elsewhere. Those who couldn't speak could hire an orator to write a speech for them, which they would then memorise and deliver as appropriate. The Greek world's acknowledged master of rhetoric, who wrote both for others and for himself, was the Athenian statesman Demosthenes (384 – 322 BC). He was remembered for centuries afterwards as the exemplar of the ideal orator; he was even looked up to by the magisterial Roman orator Cicero, whom we are about to meet. In Chapter 1, we came across an example of Greek public oratory in the form of Pericles' Funeral Speech. As we noted, Thucydides' version was probably to a large extent an invention of his own, but set-piece funeral speeches for those who had fallen in battle were an important part of the real-life Athenian oratorical tradition.

The subject of oratory was written on at length by both Plato and Aristotle. Aristotle's ideas, as set out in his treatise *Rhetoric*, still remain influential today. It is to him that we owe the classic distinction of oratory into three species: *forensic* (law-court speeches), *deliberative* (speeches for or against a political proposal) and *epideictic* (speeches of praise or blame). Greek intellectuals fiercely debated the nature of rhetoric and its proper uses. On one side, Plato famously rejected the legitimacy of rhetoric in the sense of skilful playing with words, divorced from philosophical and ethical truth. On the other side were the Sophists, the intellectual radicals whom we briefly met in Chapter

181

5 and who worried conservatives by teaching rhetoric outside the context of traditional social values. While the Sophists did not have a unified outlook, there was an undercurrent of subversiveness in their activities which is well captured in the famous claim of Protagoras, one of their number, that he could make the weaker argument the stronger. This is the origin of the modern idea of "sophistry". In between Plato and the Sophists was the anti-democratic politician and educator Isocrates, who favoured striking some kind of balance between oratory and philosophy.

One of the best known Sophists was Gorgias (483 – 375 BC). Gorgias is famous for starring in a rather ill-tempered dialogue written by Plato (called, naturally enough, the *Gorgias*) and for writing a speech known as the *Encomium of Helen.* I mentioned in Chapter 2 that Helen of Troy was traditionally blamed for starting the Trojan War because she deserted Agamemnon to elope with Paris. Gorgias sought to defend Helen from this charge, and his speech is a superficially serious piece of forensic oratory. Yet the *Encomium* itself refers to the power and deceptiveness of persuasion, as exercised by Paris on Helen, and Gorgias ends the speech by referring to it as his *paignion*, "plaything". It is perhaps not difficult to see why this sort of thing went down badly with a profoundly serious philosopher like

Plato, and with conservative opinion more generally. There is a parallel to be drawn with modern concerns about political spin and media management replacing honest, substantive debate.

Greek oratorical education had migrated to Rome by the second century BC, although not without some opposition. Roman traditionalists even made attempts to legally persecute Greek teachers of rhetoric and their Roman imitators. In the end, a typically Roman moralised ideal of oratory took root – although, as we will see, it was rivalled by a more "Sophistic" take on the subject. The Roman oratorical tradition can perhaps be traced back to the austere old statesman Cato the Elder – the brothel guy from Chapter 4 – who famously described the orator as *"vir bonus dicendi peritus"*, "a good man skilled at speaking". That said, Cato was no fan of Greek rhetorical flummery, and he also gave the laconic rhetorical advice *"rem tene, verba sequentur"*, "hold to the subject, the words will follow".

Oratory became a key accomplishment of a Roman gentleman. It was intimately associated with law and politics – which were, together with soldiering, the pre-eminent careers for upper-class Romans. Take, for example, this revealing passage from the historian Livy, in which he is talking about a politician called Publius Licinius Crassus:

He was considered to be most eloquent, whether he was plying his talents for persuasion and dissuasion in pleading cases, in the Senate or before the people. He was very knowledgeable on religious law; and in addition his tenure as Consul had given him a share in military glory. (30.1.5-6)

In a nutshell, a successful career in Roman public life meant being good at two things – speaking and fighting.

The very best orators didn't even need to be good at fighting. This was certainly true of the greatest of all Roman orators, the lawyer and politician Marcus Tullius Cicero (106 – 43 BC). The middle-class Cicero was something of an upstart in the ranks of the Roman élite. A more authentically blue-blooded colleague, Metellus Nepos, is said to have taunted him by asking him who his father was; Cicero replied that Nepos' mother had made it more difficult for him to answer the same question (Plutarch, *Cicero,* 23.9). Yet in spite of his relatively undistinguished origins – or perhaps because of them – Cicero was a political conservative.

We might pause here to give a couple of examples of Cicero's oratory. What follows is the final passage of his *Second Philippic*, a speech written to condemn the real-life Mark Antony when the latter was in the process of destroying the Roman Republic (and was about to have Cicero himself murdered):

Take time to reflect, I beg you. Consider those from whom you are descended, not those with whom you are consorting now.... In any event, see to your own affairs – I will declare what I am going to do. I defended the Republic as a young man; I will not desert it in my old age. I scorned the swords of Catiline; I will not be afraid of yours. No, indeed, I will willingly offer my body, if by my death the freedom of the state can be restored, so that finally the birth-pangs of the Roman people bring forth that with which they have now so long been in labour. Indeed, if nearly twenty years ago I said in this very temple that death could not come too soon for a man who had been Consul, how much more truly may I say it now that I am an old man! For me, Senators, death is now even something to be hoped for, after I have obtained all that I have obtained and achieved all that I have achieved. I hope only for these two things: first, that in dying I might leave the Roman people free – the immortal gods can give nothing greater to me than this –

AN INTRODUCTION TO CLASSICS

and second, that every man may have what he deserves from his service to the Republic.

This short passage is filled with classic and obvious rhetorical tricks – the personal appeal, the repeated parallelisms, the use of metaphor, the stirring of patriotic and republican sentiment. It also refers to Cicero's own finest hour, which he could never resist bringing up – his suppression of a left-wing *coup d'état* by the populist politician Catiline in 63 BC, the year in which Cicero had served as Consul. The great man even wrote a self-congratulatory poem about it in three books entitled *On My Consulship*. Modesty and humility were not Roman virtues.

Our second example of Cicero's oratory comes from the opening of his *First Speech Against Catiline*. This was the very speech – polished for publication, of course – with which he had confronted Catiline in the Senate all those years before. Its opening passage is one of the best-known pieces of rhetoric in Western history:

For how long, Catiline, are you going to abuse our patience? For how much longer will this madness of yours mock us? When will your unbridled audacity cease to flaunt itself? The night-time guard on the

Palatine Hill, the city watchmen, the fear of the people, the union of all good men, the fact that the Senate has assembled in this heavily defended location, the faces and expressions of these men – does all this leave you unmoved? Do you not realise that your plans have been revealed? Do you not see that your conspiracy is already thwarted, and is known to all these men? Which of us do you think does not know what you were doing last night, or the night before, where you were, whom you were meeting with and what you were planning? What an age, what behaviour! The Senate knows all this, the Consul sees it – yet this man still lives. Lives? More than that, he comes into the Senate, takes part in public business, and marks and chooses each and every one of us with his eyes for slaughter.

The rhetorical features of this passage aren't difficult to spot. The aggressively hostile tone, the repeated rhetorical questions, the phrases piled on top of one another, the memorable image of Catiline silently marking out his senatorial colleagues for death. And, most of all, the famous exclamation *"O tempora, o mores!"*, which I have translated rather feebly as "What an age, what behaviour!"'. It has since become the cry of the disaffected and the middle-aged down the centuries.

For Cicero, however, oratory was not just technical skill with words. It was a whole set of accomplishments. Nor did it consist only of being naturally bright. It was also a matter of intellectual and emotional knowledge which required study and training. What was being said was even more important than how one said it. Cicero wrote several works in which he set out his views on the subject of oratory and the orator, the best of which is probably the *De Oratore*, or *On the Orator*.

The *De Oratore* takes the form of a dialogue, like the works of Plato. The case for oratory is put primarily by Lucius Licinius Crassus, a descendant of the Publius Licinius Crassus whom Livy wrote about, and who in real life had been Cicero's own teacher. Oratory, says Crassus, is a powerful and noble means of influencing people and society for good ends. It has allowed men to found societies and to rise up from barbarism. It is the art of the statesman. This is the classically Roman "high" view of the orator's craft, which has its origins at least as far back as Plato and the anti-Sophistic school in Greece.

There is a certain fascination in receiving a masterclass from Cicero's own teacher. Crassus prescribes studies in diverse areas, including law, philosophy, history and poetry. Specific recommended techniques for practising one's rhetorical skills include composing written speeches; translating Greek speeches into Latin; studying the techniques of actors; and learning by heart the works of both Latin and Greek writers. Crassus advises that the would-be orator should become adept at constructing arguments: "Argue every issue from the opposing sides. On every topic, draw out and articulate whatever arguments can be viewed as plausible." As to the practical business of making a speech, he outlines the five classic steps, which went back to the Greeks: decide what points to make; arrange them in order; adorn them with rhetorical style; memorise them; and then deliver them effectively.

What Crassus says does not go unchallenged. In particular, Cicero puts a contrary view into the mouth of another character called Marcus Antonius (the grandfather of *the* Mark Antony, the one who had Cicero killed). According to Antonius, Crassus has an unduly elevated view of oratory – surely it's more about winning arguments than high statesmanship? Antonius accordingly criticises Crassus' recommended course of education as unnecessarily burdensome and academic. For his part, Crassus complains: "You restrict the orator from a huge and immense field to a tiny circle". This disagreement reflected wider debates in Roman society on the place of oratory and rhetorical education, which were in turn a continuation of the debates on the relationship between philosophy and rhetoric which had raged in the heyday of classical Athens. The views which Cicero put into Crassus' mouth did not represent an uncontroversial consensus position. Cicero himself may not have entirely agreed with them. He was certainly not above descending from the lofty heights on occasion: he apparently boasted that in one court case he had used his oratorical skills to "pour darkness over the judges" (Quintilian, 2.17.21).

Controversial or not, the "high" view of oratory survived and continued to win influential adherents. It was quite unremarkable for a Roman in the decades after Cicero's lifetime to claim that oratory was an honourable and important accomplishment which was to be cultivated by means of a broad education. At first sight, this might seem a little odd. It might be thought that such ideas would not survive Cicero's own generation. It was one thing to extol the virtues of oratory in Republican Rome – or, indeed, in democratic Athens – but the end of the Republic might be expected to have changed things. Didn't the advent of a monarchical political system mean that public debate was replaced by imperial patronage? It has been argued that there are indications even in the *De Oratore* that

Cicero realised that the idealised "high" view of the orator and his craft was flawed or becoming obsolete.

Romans in the early imperial era did appear to agree that oratory had undergone a decline, and they sometimes attributed this to the new political conditions. One writer who adopted this thesis was our friend the historian Tacitus, in his *Dialogue on Orators* (which was modelled on Cicero's *De Oratore*). One of the characters in the dialogue is still able to put forward an old-fashioned Ciceronian conception of the paramount importance of oratory, but it is clear that Tacitus himself thought that things had moved on. Having said that, at least some of the complaints that we find in our sources about the decline of oratory arose out of typical Roman moralistic good-old-days-ism. The explanations proffered for the decline of oratory included the laziness of the young, declining educational standards and growing effeminacy.

Notwithstanding such criticism, the fact is that oratory survived under the imperial monarchy and prospered to a perhaps surprising degree. Then as now, an authoritarian state still needed politicians and lawyers who were endowed with certain oratorical gifts. The advent of the imperial regime had removed the possibility of advocating a programme openly hostile to that of the Emperor, but the Emperor couldn't do everything himself and institutions such as the law courts continued to function. In a similar way, Greek rhetoric had survived the fall of democracy and the rise of Alexander the Great and his monarchic successors.

One of the stern old Romans who thought that the art of oratory was going to the dogs was the orator and writer Seneca the Elder (c.55 BC – 39 AD). He was the father of the Stoic philosopher and playwright Seneca the Younger, whom we met in the last chapter. At the request of his sons, Seneca composed two books on oratory, containing practice exercises and setting out the ways in which various famous orators had tackled them. Such exercises were an established part of the Roman rhetorical scene: they could be set by teachers to train their pupils, or they could be tackled by accomplished speakers in front of an audience as a form of live entertainment. Seneca the Elder's first book consists of *Controversiae*, or speeches in court cases, and the second comprises *Suasoriae*, or speeches of persuasion. The distinction between these two genres was a standard feature of Roman oratorical training. In each case, the scenarios on which the exercises were based were partly taken from history or mythology and partly made up. Seneca apparently dictated the two works from memory in advanced old age.

Many of the *Controversiae* relate to family dynamics and kinship, with the issues at stake including the duties of family members, the chastity of women and rights of inheritance. Other

Controversiae relate to public affairs. The themes used in the exercises are interesting in their own right. The scenarios are artificial, and the laws involved may have been invented, but they do shed some light on Roman social attitudes. The law says that a victim of a rape can choose either to marry her attacker (she would otherwise be unmarriageable) or to have him executed. A man rapes two women in one night; one asks for marriage, the other execution; what is to be done? A married couple live in a country ruled by a tyrant; the wife undergoes torture for the sake of her husband; he subsequently divorces her because she is infertile. Can she bring a lawsuit against him? A man kills a tyrant by burning down a house which he is visiting, and receives a reward as a result. Can the owner of the house sue him for damages for arson? A man is desperately ill and asks his slave to give him poison. Should the slave be executed if he refuses to kill his master? A son with a history of trouble with his father is caught secretly preparing poison; he claims that he was intending to drink the poison himself. Should he be convicted of attempting to murder his father?

There is even an early example of welfare fraud. Ten young men who have spent all their inheritances decide that one of them, chosen by lot, will be blinded and will accordingly receive a payment from the state of 1,000 denarii. They go through with the plan. Should the payment be made? The strangest scenario is this one:

A good-looking young man made a bet that he would go out in public dressed in women's clothes. He did so, and he was raped by ten other young men. He prosecuted them for assault and had them convicted. He was prohibited by the magistrate from speaking in public and is prosecuting the magistrate for doing injury to him. (5.6)

The *Suasoriae* are more heavily dependent on topics from history and mythology. Should Cicero burn his writings to save his life, if that is what Mark Antony demands? Should the 300 Spartans at Thermopylae retreat like the other Greeks? Should Agamemnon sacrifice Iphigeneia? The arguments advanced in this last case are interesting. Some are arguments of principle – for example, killing one's own child is too high a price to pay in order to avenge an adultery. However, others are rationalistic arguments which dispute whether the gods are in fact responsible for weather conditions. Roman orators were prepared to attack the basic premise that Artemis required a sacrifice from Agamemnon. After all, if the gods controlled the weather, they wouldn't have given Paris a safe passage when he was fleeing to Troy with Helen, would they? Agamemnon should sit tight: the winds are bound to drop eventually. Not even Euripides tried to pull off anything like this.

Seneca the Younger clearly learnt a thing or two about rhetoric from his dad: we have already noted the oratorical style that may be seen in his plays and other writings. His style was not to everybody's taste, however. Among his critics was one Marcus Fabius Quintilianus, a fellow migrant from Roman Spain, who is generally known as Quintilian (c.35 – c.100 AD). Quintilian was the grand master of Roman oratorical education, a man fit to be mentioned in the same breath as Cicero, whom he leant on heavily as a source (although he did not slavishly follow his ideas). His masterpiece was the *Institutio Oratoria* (*Oratorical Education*). This consists of 12 lengthy books, much of which are taken up with technical instruction. We also have two collections of *Declamations* which are ascribed to him, and which are comparable to Seneca the Elder's collections of exercises. These may not have been composed by Quintilian himself, however; in any event, they are badly edited.

Quintilian was another advocate of the "high" view of oratory. Like Cicero's Crassus, he saw oratory as a tool for creating civilisation itself; and the old idea of the orator as a statesman persists in the *Institutio Oratoria*. Quintilian quotes Cato the Elder's description of an orator as "a good man skilled at speaking" – and indeed he takes the idea further. "I do not only say that an orator should be a good man," he writes, "but even that only a good man can become an orator" (12.1.3).

Quintilian's orator also needed to be a man of learning. Quintilian recommended that a father should start thinking about his son's oratorical education as soon as he was born. Most people have intellectual ability, he says, and what is lacking is education. A boy should be taught Greek, but not – as was often the case in Roman high society – exclusively Greek with no Latin. The study of literature should start with Homer and Virgil, not neglecting earlier Latin authors: "purity, certainly, and manliness, if I can put it that way, are to be found with them, since we have descended into every luxurious vice even in our style of language" (1.8.9). Other studies should include music, geometry, astronomy and law.

Quintilian's influence was, and continues to be, immense. He influenced figures as diverse as St Augustine, Petrarch and John Stuart Mill. He advocated something like what we would call child-centred education, as well as lifelong learning. In the near term, he had a more immediate influence on his own pupils. These may have included Tacitus, although the latter broke with

Quintilian's views in his *Dialogue on Orators*. They certainly included Pliny the Younger (c.61 – c.112 AD). Pliny was a lawyer, judge and public servant. Starting his legal career at 18, he inherited a considerable fortune from his uncle – Pliny the Elder, the religious sceptic whom we met in Chapter 5. He went on to become a personal friend of the Emperor Trajan.

Pliny's sole surviving piece of oratory is a speech known as the *Panegyric*. This is a long speech of praise in honour of Trajan which incorporates Pliny's own ideas about what an ideal emperor should be. These ideas are anchored in traditional Roman virtues: gravity, piety, humanity, self-control, and so on. They also have a political dimension: the thrust of the advice is that Trajan should behave not like some of his arrogant, autocratic predecessors, but instead like a fellow member of the senatorial class (which he did, to some extent – Trajan was one of the "good" emperors). The *Panegyric* is an important piece of prose. Indeed, it is the only complete speech in Latin to survive between the works of Cicero and 289 AD, when we have a speech composed for the Emperor Maximian's birthday. However, Pliny is principally remembered not for the *Panegyric* but for his collection of published correspondence. It is always interesting to read someone else's letters, and Pliny's letters offer a unique glimpse into the life of a man who had completed the traditional course of oratorical training and had gone on to follow a distinguished career of public speaking and public service.

Pliny was a well-connected member of Roman high society, and his correspondents included Tacitus and two other prominent historians, Suetonius and Fabius Rusticus. He also mentions the poets Martial and Silius Italicus. But then oratory was an upper-class, male realm. It was assumed that the would-be orator's family would have the money and leisure to have him taught the art, and that in later life he would have the opportunity to practise it in the courts and elsewhere. Not all of Pliny's friends were major public figures, however. Other addressees of his letters comprised friends, colleagues and family members, including women.

In the letters, Pliny talks about bereavements, dinner parties, the art of oratory, the affairs of the Senate and events in his own life. He recounts ghost stories and provides a couple of well-known descriptions of the eruption of Vesuvius in 79 AD. He complains about orators in the Centumviral Court, the law court in which he spent most of his professional life, hiring claques to applaud their speeches. Some of his letters are poignant. Here is one that he wrote to his wife, Calpurnia:

It is unbelievable how tightly desire for you holds me bound. The cause, firstly, is love – and also the fact that we are not used to being apart. So I lie awake thinking of you for a great part of the night, while by day, at the times when I used to see you, my feet take me (I'm telling the complete truth) to your quarters – and then I slink back from the deserted threshold, feeling sick and sad, like a locked-out lover. There is only one time that is free from these torments, and that is when I am being worn out in the Forum and by the lawsuits of my friends. Judge what my life is like when my rest is in work and my recreation is in misery and anxiety. (7.5)

Modern readers might not have much difficulty relating to Pliny's love for his wife, but in other respects his attitudes and beliefs were quite foreign (if typically Roman). He shows us the same mixture of the familiar and the alien as the ancient world as a whole. If he was a good husband, he was also a man who had no problem with, say, slavery or social inequality. Nevertheless, he did become irritated at displays of what he considered to be inappropriately hierarchical behaviour, as the following somewhat self-satisfied letter shows. The letter also offers a fascinating glimpse into the scene at a posh Roman dinner party:

....I, a very unsociable man, came to be dining with a certain person – a man who in his own opinion is magnificent and thrifty but in my opinion is sordid and extravagant. He served some excellent food to himself and a few others, but cheap and small portions to the rest. He had even poured out three different types of wine in small flasks – not so that people could choose which to have, but so that no-one could refuse what they were given. He gave some of them to himself and a few of the rest of us, some to his less close friends (for he has different grades of friendship), and others to his and our former slaves. A man who was reclining close to me noticed this and asked if I approved of it. I said that I didn't. "So", he said, "what practice do you follow?" "I serve the same food to everyone – I am inviting them to dine, not to be categorised. I treat them equally in all respects, since I have made them equals at my table and couch." "Even the former slaves?" "Even them, for on such an occasion I think of them as fellow diners, not as former slaves." And he said: "That must cost you a lot." "Not at all." "How can that be?" "Because it's not the case that my former slaves drink the same as me, it's that I drink the same as them." (2.6)

In another letter, Pliny boasts about freeing a slave. Again, he is clearly rather pleased with himself, but his approach to his task is refreshingly unlawyerly:

You write that Sabina, who nominated us as her executors, did not give any instructions that her slave Modestus should be set free, but that she did confer a legacy on him in these words: "To Modestus, whom I have ordered to be set free". You ask me what I think about this. I have consulted with some legal experts. Their unanimous opinion is that he is not entitled either to his freedom, because it was not expressly granted to him, or to his legacy, because it was left to him as a slave. But this seems to me to be clearly wrong, and so I think that we should act as if Sabina had written what she thought she had written. I'm sure that you will agree with my opinion, since it is your habit to adhere scrupulously to the wishes of the deceased, which for honourable executors are tantamount to a legal obligation. For to us, honour has no less force than necessity has for others. Let us therefore allow the slave to have his freedom, and let him enjoy his legacy as if Sabina had attended to everything with all due care – for

201

she took such care in choosing her executors well. (4.10)

As you can see, at his worst Pliny comes across as somewhat pompous and precious (and there are indications that his contemporaries thought the same). On the whole, however, he was a thoughtful and decent man, and he deserves to be remembered benignly.

The last of the ten Books in the collection of letters consists of correspondence between Pliny and the Emperor Trajan which dates from Pliny's special assignment as imperial legate to the troubled province of Bithynia and Pontus, in modern-day Turkey. It has been noted that Pliny seems to have been a bit too quick to ask for instructions from Trajan, who appears to be slightly annoyed in some of his replies. It is in this Book that we find a famous exchange of letters on the subject of how to deal with the new sect of *Christiani* which had appeared and which was attracting not only city-dwellers but people in the countryside too. Pliny didn't like the new movement, but he didn't consider it much of a threat to the state: "I found nothing except a perverse and extreme superstition", he reported to the Emperor, before going on to note that more people had started going to the temples again.

We may close this chapter with Pliny's own reflections on his life and career – the wistful thoughts of an orator who had stood up in court for the umpteenth time and found himself thinking of all the occasions in the past when he had done the same. It also gives some insight into the sort of men who spoke for a living in ancient Rome, and what kind of lives they led:

Very recently, when I had been speaking before the combined bench at the Centumviral Court, the memory came to me of how I had spoken in the past in the same way before the combined bench. My mind continued on this train of thought, as is a habit with me: I began to recall the men who had been my work colleagues in that court and in the other one. I was the only one left who had spoken in both courts: such has been the effect of all the vicissitudes and fragilities of human life and the fickleness of fortune. Some of those who were active back then have died, and others are in exile. Some have been persuaded to retire by age and ill health, and others are enjoying of their own volition all the blessings of leisure. Some have taken up military commands, and others have withdrawn from professional life due to their friendship with the Emperor. As for myself, how much has changed!... If you count the years, the length of time is short. If you look at what has changed, you would think that an age had passed. (4.24)

8. History Writing and Two Roman Historians

We can add the business of writing history to the long list of elements of Western culture that were invented by the Greeks and Romans. The word "history" itself comes from the Greek *historia*, "inquiry". As with so much else about the ancient world, history writing back then was both similar to and different from what modern professional historians get up to today.

Not that there is universal agreement on what it is that modern historians do, or ought to be doing. On the contrary, there is a wide-ranging philosophical debate about what history actually *is* – the issue of "historiography". A spectrum of views has emerged, ranging from the claim that history is essentially akin to the "hard" sciences like physics and chemistry to the claim that writing history is essentially no different from writing a novel. Whole books are written defending different theories. Ancient historians tended not to engage in this sort of navel-gazing (although they sometimes did so), and modern historiographical debates would have seemed rather unfamiliar to them. Their works, however, certainly do bear witness to radically different ideas about the craft of the historian: what it means to write history and how it should be done. To that extent, "history" in the ancient world was as diverse and elastic a thing as it is today.

In the beginning, "history" did not exist as a discrete discipline or genre of writing. If we take the word in its broadest sense, the Homeric epics are the first works of "history" that we possess. They do, after all, claim to recount events which happened in the past. Homeric bards were "historians" insofar as their job was to compose narratives of things which had taken place in former times; and we have seen that they explicitly saw themselves as preserving the *kleos* of great men and women. Artistic creativity naturally had its place, just as it does in history writing generally. But the original performers and audiences of the *Iliad* and the *Odyssey* would probably have regarded the epics as fundamentally being about real people and events. Indeed, as we have noted, even in our own sceptical age many scholars believe that they have an historical core.

Of course, history did eventually emerge as a separate enterprise – self-consciously scholarly, prosaic rather than poetic, concerned with evidence and causation, aiming to educate and inform as well as to entertain. Yet its boundaries always remained fuzzy. It is not always possible to make a sharp distinction between ancient works of history and works from other genres, such as poetry and rhetoric. Quintilian even referred to history in the *Institutio Oratoria* as "a kind of poetry without metre" (10.1.31). Not all Graeco-Roman historians would have agreed with this, and some might have strongly objected – but this just goes to highlight the diversity and elasticity within the field of history writing that we have already referred to.

The study and writing of history – like so much else – first flowered in classical Greece before going on to see a second springtime under the Roman Empire. We have already come across the two star Greek historians, Herodotus and Thucydides. Herodotus wrote about the Greeks' struggles with the Persians in the early 5th century BC, amongst a great many other things. Thucydides wrote about the Peloponnesian War which Athens and Sparta fought in the last third of the 5th century. Herodotus has gone down in history as hugely knowledgeable and entertaining but somewhat credulous – a storyteller rather than a scientific analyst. He is a prime example of a writer whose work comes at times closer to legend and romance than to what we might regard as "real" history. It was not for nothing that the nine books of his *History* were named after the nine Muses, the goddesses of artistic inspiration. His reputation can be summed up by two nicknames which were coined for him by other ancient writers – "The Father of History" and "The Father of Lies". Thucydides, by contrast, is remembered as a hard-headed rationalist – a soldier and statesman who wrote about war and politics and didn't have much time for gods and miracles. He deliberately distanced himself from Herodotus, and he appears to have been rather proud of his scientific approach and his ultra-realism. He is apparently still taught in university courses on international relations as a kind of ancient Henry Kissinger.

The contrast between these two men shows how very different approaches to writing about the past could end up being bracketed in the same category of "history". This is not a novel insight. It was already understood by ancient commentators. One ancient writer, a fan of the serious, rational Thucydidean approach, had this to say, quoting and paraphrasing some of Thucydides' own words:

And so Thucydides laid down the law well and distinguished between good and bad in history writing. He saw that men were greatly impressed by Herodotus, to the extent that the books [of his *History*] were named after the Muses. He therefore said that his own writings would be an asset for ever rather than a bid for short-term fame; and that one should not be indulgent towards legendary material, but should bequeath to future generations the truth about what happened. He emphasised usefulness, and said that a wise man who undertakes to write history should aim that, if ever similar events happen again, men will be able to handle those events well by studying what he has written. (Lucian, *How to Write History*, 42)

There was, then, a great deal of variety among ancient historians, as well as some fuzziness in the boundaries of history itself. It is only fair to say that the stereotyped reputations of Herodotus and Thucydides are not entirely accurate. Herodotus appears to have gone to considerable effort to travel around and interview his informants, and he tells us that he doesn't necessarily believe everything that he recounts. For his part, Thucydides is not a paragon of objectivity, not least because he was a leading participant in the war which he was writing about. His anti-democratic bias is particularly notorious. Nevertheless, Herodotus and Thucydides do each represent something important and different about the business of writing history, both then and now. History has always been a broad church.

I have brought up the two Greek giants because of their seminal importance in the history of history. I strongly advise you to read at least one of them. Try the first book of Herodotus (who has been particularly well served by English translators) and then the first book of Thucydides. The contrast between the two men will be striking. This chapter will not be looking at them in any further detail – but it will be looking at examples of the differing models of history writing which they represented. In particular, I want to take a look at two later writers: two Roman historians, one well-known and one obscure. Taking a look at their work will allow us to compare and contrast their different approaches, and also the similarities and differences between their works and modern ways of writing history.

*

The first Roman historian whom I want to look at is Livy, the stolid old moralist who thought that modern Rome was going to the dogs.

Livy or Titus Livius (c.60 BC – 17 AD) was one of the most popular and best loved historians of the ancient world. His admirers included such luminaries as Seneca the Elder, Quintilian and Tacitus. In one of his letters, our friend Pliny the Younger tells a story about how one of Livy's fans travelled all the way to Rome from Gades (modern Cadiz in Spain) just to see him. His reputation remained high in later times too, and he was well regarded by Dante and Machiavelli. He was an accomplished prose stylist, and he remains very readable today. On the other hand, as we will see, he has a reputation for taking liberties with historical accuracy.

Livy's history of Rome, *From the Foundation of the City*, was enormous. It consisted of 142 books, 35 of which still survive today. In this chapter, we will be looking at Book 1 – the book which deals with the period up to the establishment of the Roman Republic in 509 BC.

Long before Livy's time, the Romans had come to believe that they were descended from the legendary heroes of Greek mythology. This rather strange idea originally came from the Greeks themselves, but it was taken up by the Romans with some eagerness. It allowed Rome, a relatively young nation, to link its history and destiny with the venerable and prestigious culture of the Greek world. The Romans were not just spear-throwing upstarts, barbarians from an obscure town in central Italy: they were the inheritors of the rich and respected traditions of the Homeric heroes. Interestingly, mediaeval writers in Britain tried to pull a similar stunt, linking the origins of the *British* with the made-up character *Brutus*, a hero of Trojan blood.

And so, driven by Roman cultural anxiety, Livy takes the Trojan War as his point of departure. He tells of how the Trojan hero Aeneas migrated to Italy after Troy was captured – the same story that Virgil would later tell in his *Aeneid.* Generations passed, and in due course two twins, Romulus and Remus, were born to Aeneas' family line, which had by now become the royal house of a city called Alba Longa. This is clearly an attempt to graft an indigenous Roman legend, the simple story of Romulus and Remus, on to the mythical traditions of the Greek world. Livy and other Roman writers knew that the Trojan War would have taken place long before the traditional date for Rome's foundation (753 BC), and so they bridged the gap with the mythical royal dynasty of Alba Longa.

Livy tells the famous story of how Romulus and Remus were suckled by a she-wolf. When they reached adulthood, Romulus founded the city of Rome and became its first king – although in the process he quarrelled with Remus and killed him. Romulus gave laws to his new city, as well as state institutions such as the Senate. He also enlarged its population. Livy recounts the rather disturbing story of the "rape of the Sabine women". The Romans staged a festival with games; invited the neighbouring peoples, including the Sabines, to attend; and used the occasion to carry off their daughters by force ("rape" in Latin, or *raptus*, principally meant "carrying off" rather than sexual violence). War ensued – but the Romans and their Sabine foes were separated by the captured women, who declared that they were now all kinsfolk and should stop fighting each other. Peace duly broke out, and the infant Roman state was off and running.

Rome developed an elective monarchy, and Livy reports that Romulus was succeeded by a Sabine man by the name of Numa Pompilius. Numa is portrayed as a stereotypically pious fellow who founded many of Rome's religious rites and priesthoods. The saintly old buffer was succeeded by Tullus Hostilius, an equally stereotypical warrior figure, who waged war against Rome's neighbours. The fourth king was Ancus Marcius, a shadowy figure whom Livy describes as a kind of synthesis of his pious and warlike predecessors.

Modern scholars would regard most of this as legendary. No-one seriously argues that Romulus was a real person, and Numa and Tullus are clearly symbolic archetypes rather than historical figures. At the most, their names may perhaps represent authentic memories of the names of early Roman chieftains. But the next three kings of Rome – who also happen to be the last kings of the city – are often thought to have a claim to be genuine historical figures. This is so even though there is clearly a lot of legendary material in Livy's account of them.

The first of these "real" kings was Tarquin I. His origins lay in the Greek world (note the recurring motif) and he migrated to Rome from Etruria, a powerful nation based in modern-day Tuscany. The Etruscans, as they are called, were a strong influence on early Rome, and Livy is right to see them as playing a major role in the development of the growing city. Tarquin I was succeeded by Servius Tullius, who introduced the "census" – the financial and military classification system used by the later Romans. This system does indeed seem to date from pre-Republican times, and it may well have been devised by a king called Servius Tullius.

The final king of the line was Tarquin II, the son or grandson of Tarquin I, who seized power from Servius in a *coup d'état* and ruled Rome as a tyrant. Livy attributes to Tarquin II a well known story that was originally told about an archaic Greek ruler called Thrasybulus. Tarquin's son, Sextus, sent a messenger to Tarquin to ask his advice on how to govern the town of Gabii. In reply, Tarquin silently struck off the heads of the tallest poppies in his garden. The messenger was baffled about what this meant, but Livy assures us that his son got the point.

Another story about Tarquin II is worth mentioning. The tyrant arrived late to a meeting of the lords of the cities of Latium (modern Lazio), the region in which Rome was situated. He excused himself on the pretext that he had been asked to rule on a quarrel between a father and a son. An enemy of his, Turnus Herdonius of Aricia, replied that such a case could easily be settled with a few words: "if you do not obey your father, it will be the worse for you" (1.50).

Tarquin II ends up being deposed and exiled by his nephew, Brutus (no relation to the Brutus who was supposed to have founded Britain). Livy explains how this happened by means of another well known story – the rape of Lucretia. A group of princes, including Tarquin's son Sextus, were getting drunk together one night while out on campaign. They fell to arguing about whose wife was the best, and they ended up going back home to find out. Most of the wives turned out to be partying, but Lucretia, the spouse of a man named Collatinus, was at home with her slave-girls, working her wool like a dutiful Roman wife. Sextus later returned and raped her. In anguish, she told her male relatives, including Brutus, what had happened. This is how one translator of Livy rendered the scene, which comes closer to melodrama than what we might recognise as history:

"Is all well?" she replied, "Far from it; for what can be well with a woman when she has lost her honour? The print of a strange man, Collatinus, is in your bed. Yet my body only has been violated; my heart is guiltless, as death shall be my witness. But pledge your right hands and your words that the adulterer shall not go unpunished. Sextus Tarquinius is he that last night returned hostility for hospitality, and brought ruin on me, and on himself no less – if you are men – when he worked his pleasure with me." They give their pledges, every man in turn. They seek to comfort her, sick at heart as she is, by diverting the blame from her who was forced to the doer of the wrong. They tell her it is the mind that sins, not the body; and that, where purpose has been wanting, there is no guilt. "It is for you to determine," she answers, "what is due to him; for my own part, though I acquit myself of the sin, I do not absolve myself from punishment; nor in time to come shall ever unchaste woman live through the example of Lucretia." Taking a knife which she had concealed beneath her dress, she plunged it into her heart, and sinking forward upon the wound, died as she fell. The wail for the dead was raised by her husband and her father." (1.58; trans. B.O.Foster)

No wonder the Lucretia story has provided fertile material for writers and artists from Shakespeare to Benjamin Britten.

The expulsion of the Tarquins spells the end of Rome's period of kingly rule and the beginning of the Republic. Livy famously describes the Republican constitution as "a government of laws rather than men" (2.1) – a phrase which was later borrowed by the American revolutionaries, who saw themselves as the inheritors of the Roman Republican tradition. Brutus, who was probably a real person, became one of the first Consuls of the Republic. Centuries later, his reputation as an enemy of tyrants led to his descendant, Marcus Junius Brutus, becoming a leading figure in the plot to assassinate Julius Caesar. (Caesar, incidentally, didn't really say *"Et tu, Brute?"*, although he might have used the Greek phrase *"Kai su, teknon?"*, "You too, my son?")

As I mentioned, Livy's work is often found wanting by modern scholars. It may be said that he lacked the critical skills of modern historians, or even the *desire* to be critical. There is no doubt that he was a fluent and entertaining writer, just like Herodotus – indeed, Quintilian expressly compared him to

Herodotus (*Institutio Oratoria*, 10.1.101). But he was arguably more interested in rhetoric, storytelling and moralising than in strict Thucydidean accuracy. He did not (it is said) have much interest in restricting himself to reporting matters which were well attested by reliable evidence. This is why he reports fantastic myths and legends alongside events which were probably more or less factual.

There is undoubtedly some truth in these criticisms, and they do help to illustrate our earlier point about how history writing could shade into poetry and rhetoric. Livy does recount stories which are clearly legendary, and which would be more at home in the *Odyssey* than in Niall Ferguson or David Starkey. A random example of this would be the tale that King Servius Tullius' head burst into flames when he was a child. One particular concern for Livy was to provide origin-stories for Roman customs and institutions – aetiologies, as they are known in the jargon – even when the stories are clearly wishful thinking. Hence, for example, he attributes various features of the Roman state to Romulus as the founding father, and various elements of Roman religion to Numa Pompilius as the archetypal Mr Pious. In more general terms, Livy was somewhat lacking in historical imagination: he seems to regard early Rome as being little different from the Rome of his own day, rather than as a small, rather primitive, semi-tribal settlement. Finally, as we saw back in Chapter 1, he explicitly saw history as having the purpose of furnishing morally improving examples of behaviour, good and bad, to his readers.

Nevertheless, on closer inspection, there is less to the case for the prosecution than meets the eye. Even where the criticisms of Livy are valid, they often hit equally hard at present-day historians. It is surprisingly difficult even for sophisticated modern scholars to distinguish myth from history in the narratives of early Rome, and it seems a bit harsh to condemn Livy for being credulous when he was essentially a gifted amateur who lacked our modern academic resources and knowledge of archaeology. It is also a well-worn cliché that all historians have some form of bias. Livy's overt moralising may currently be unfashionable, but in pursuing his chosen agenda he wasn't doing anything in principle that modern historians don't do. At least he had the candour to admit what he was up to.

There is, moreover, a positive case to be made for seeing Livy as having at least some of the traits that are prized in modern academic historians. He may have been an amateur, but he *was* concerned with accuracy, and he not infrequently *does* get it right, both broadly (e.g. the Etruscans heavily influenced early Rome; the city probably was ruled by the Tarquin family) and in detail (he quotes what appear to be genuine archaic legal and religious formulae). He knew what a legend (*fabula*) was, and he recognised that it was different from real history. There is a definite odour of rationalism in some of what he says, even if he doesn't take it as far as the likes of Thucydides (or even the likes of Niall Ferguson). He explicitly accepts that the legends relating to the times before Rome's foundation – such as the story that Romulus was the son of the god Mars – are factually dubious, although he says that they are nevertheless worthy of Rome's greatness. He reports a theory promoted by some other writers that the legend of the wolf (*lupa* in Latin) suckling Romulus and Remus might have grown up due to the twins being raised by a prostitute (also *lupa* in Latin).

This brings us on to another point. Livy repeatedly notes the existence of alternative accounts of events, and he shows himself to be well capable of making rational assessments of the various claims that reached him. Some earlier writers had attempted to argue that the pious Numa Pompilius had been a pupil of Pythagoras, the great Greek scholar and occultist (Pythagoras is mostly remembered today for his theorem about triangles, but he was more of a religious guru than a mathematician). Livy is sure that such claims are wrong, and he tells us why:

It is wrongly said, in the absence of any other candidate, that Numa's teacher was Pythagoras of Samos. But it is known that Pythagoras lived when Servius Tullius was King of Rome, more than a hundred years later. He gathered a group of young man eager to study with him on the far southern coast of Italy, around Metapontum, Heraclea and Croton. Even if he had lived at this time, how could the Sabines [Numa's tribe of origin] have heard about him at such a distance? And by what common language could he have encouraged any of them to want to study with him? With whose protection could one man have made the journey through so many peoples with different languages and customs? (1.18)

This is an interesting insight into Livy's thought processes. In similarly rationalistic vein, he is unwilling to believe the tradition that King Numa had nighttime trysts with a goddess called Egeria. Livy takes the view that Numa made this stuff up in order to impress his primitive subjects.

In addition, there is a political awareness to be seen in Livy's narratives. As I mentioned in Chapter 1, the Emperor Augustus suspected him of harbouring Republican sympathies and of being an opponent of Augustus' adoptive father Julius

Caesar. The books in which Livy wrote about the history of his own lifetime have annoyingly been lost, but his political awareness occasionally comes through even in the legendary material in Book 1. At one point, Livy says that it is impossible to decide at this distance whether Aeneas' son and heir was born in Troy to his first wife Creusa or in Italy to his second wife Lavinia, "for who could affirm for certain a matter so ancient?" (1.3). The answer is that Julius Caesar's family could and did affirm precisely this matter, since they maintained that Aeneas' heir was the conveniently named Julus, who was born to Creusa in Troy. Livy also reports two alternative versions of Romulus' fate: he was either taken up by the gods into heaven or torn to pieces by his own senators because he had fallen out with them, despite his popularity with the common people and the soldiers. There are obvious echoes here of the demise of Julius Caesar – a popular hero who was assassinated by his senatorial colleagues and was worshipped as a god. Just in case the reader fails to get the point, Livy recounts that the witness who testified that the divine Romulus appeared to him after his ascension was a man called Proculus Julius.

*

The second Roman historian whom I want to look at happened to be a personal acquaintance of Julius Caesar – or, to give him his full name, Gaius Julius Caesar (Roman citizens had three names – a forename or *praenomen*, a clan name or *nomen*, and an individual family name or *cognomen*). Perhaps surprisingly, we don't know what our writer's name was: he is the anonymous author of a work entitled *De Bello Africo*, or *On the African War*.

The African War was the penultimate campaign of Caesar's civil wars. This was a series of conflicts which began in January 49 BC, when Caesar famously ordered his troops across the River Rubicon from his province of Cisalpine Gaul (where he was allowed to be) into Italy (where he wasn't). The conflict was fought between the Caesarian forces and the "Pompeians", or followers of the great Roman statesman Pompey (Gnaeus Pompeius). In the febrile world of late Republican politics, Caesar was aligned with the *Populares* or populist party, while Pompey was aligned with the *Optimates* or aristocratic party.

The Pompeians may be seen as being among the last defenders of the old Republic and its free constitution. There is accordingly a temptation for the modern reader to take the side of the Pompeians against the Caesarians – but this could be a mistake. Pompey and his friends had all the best slogans about liberty and constitutional rule, but the common people of Rome may have seen things differently. Caesar was a genuinely popular figure, and the "liberty" which the Pompeians were defending was primarily the liberty of the senatorial élite to carry on running the state as they saw fit. Caesar's later assassination may have been not so much a noble deliverance from tyranny as an aristocratic plot which went down badly with the common people. To digress briefly, it may be suggested in similar vein that "bad" emperors from later times like Nero were "bad" mostly from the perspective of the upper-class politicians whose interests were threatened by them. Ordinary Romans may have liked them and benefited from their policies.

Caesar himself wrote accounts of other parts of the civil wars, as well as a famous account of his war to conquer Gaul. In these works, he proves himself to be a master of clear and direct prose style – even Cicero complimented him on this score. This is why his *De Bello Gallico* (*On the Gallic War*) was for generations a standard school text for Latin learners. This is the one which begins with the words *"Gallia est omnis divisa in partes tres"*, "Gaul as a whole is divided into three parts". In fact, Caesar's prose style is so accomplished that the reader has to consciously remember that she is reading not a neutral account of Caesar's campaigns but a set of political memoirs.

The author of *On the African War* was not, by contrast, an accomplished stylist, although his prose is at least reasonably clear. His identity was unknown even in antiquity. Some scholars have argued that he was a famous contemporary historian, such as Sallust or Asinius Pollio, but this is not likely. That he was a soldier of some sort is fairly obvious from the way in which he carefully describes the composition of forces and military manoeuvres. The work seems to have started life as some sort of campaign diary.

The author makes no claim to be impartial. He repeatedly writes in praise of Caesar, and at one point he takes it upon himself to rebut criticisms of Caesar's tactics which were going around the troops. When writing about the weakness of Caesar's forces, he has the audacity to try to make it look like it's the *Pompeians'* fault that they aren't on top form:

> For the reasons which I have mentioned, Caesar was worried and became slower and more deliberate, and departed from his old swift manner of waging war. This was not surprising: his forces were accustomed to fighting on flat land in Gaul, against Gauls, men who are open and not at all deceitful [this is the French, remember], and who are accustomed to fight using

courage rather than tricks. Now, however, Caesar had to work to accustom his soldiers to learn the tricks, ambushes and designs of the enemy, and what could fittingly be adopted and what avoided. (73)

He was an eyewitness to meetings with Caesar, and he had access to some of Caesar's thoughts and motives, albeit not in all cases. He was probably a junior officer of some sort.

In spite of the rather grand title of the book, the campaign was not a general African war. Most of the action takes place within a relatively small area of north-eastern Tunisia. For most of the time, Caesar only has a small force, including many new recruits, and he is faced with serious opposition from the Pompeian side. At one point, even the experienced troops are so nervous that Caesar has to instruct them in basic combat techniques. As for the enemy, Pompey himself is dead by now, and the leading Pompeian commander is Scipio (the descendant of the Roman hero Scipio Africanus, the man who defeated Hannibal's elephants). Scipio is assisted by a talented general called Labienus, and also by Juba, the King of Numidia (in modern-day Algeria), who is allied to the Pompeian side.

As the passage quoted above makes clear, along with other parts of the book, the Roman armies were already multicultural and multinational by this point in history. Both Caesar and the Pompeians have Gauls and Germans in their ranks, including volunteers. In addition, Caesar has Spaniards and Scipio has Numidians and other Africans. There is an obvious irony here to the extent that the Roman civil wars were fought, won and lost by non-Romans.

The book begins with Caesar mustering his forces at Lilybaeum (modern Marsala) in Sicily. The great man remains optimistic in the face of reports of how strong the enemy is. We are told:

> After completing several full-day marches, and without wasting a day, Caesar arrived at Lilybaeum on 17 December. He immediately made clear that he wanted to embark on board ship, although he had no more than one legion of new recruits and barely 600 cavalry. He pitched his tent next to the shore itself, so that the waves were beating near to it. He did this with the intention that no-one should expect to have any rest and that everyone should be prepared every hour of every day. (1)

Caesar sets sail on 25 December 47 BC, and duly arrives at Hadrumentum (modern-day Sousse in Tunisia), where there is an enemy garrison. According to the author, Caesar forbids his troops to loot the town. In any event, however, the town is well defended and Caesar has insufficient forces to attack it. The Caesarians retreat and come under attack themselves, but they put up a valiant defence. In the course of the fighting, the author reports that fewer than 30 of Caesar's Gaulish horsemen put 2,000 African horsemen to flight.

Caesar now moves around a bit and sends for reinforcements. The author relates that he is desirous that his troops should not pillage the countryside. The campaign is not going especially well for him, but he manages to put a brave face on things:

They saw that they were landed in Africa with a small force, and one composed of new recruits, not all of whom had yet disembarked, and that they faced large forces and the numberless cavalry of a treacherous nation [the Numidians]. They could not see any consolation at hand or any help in the counsels of their comrades – except in the face of the commander himself, in his energy and his amazing good humour; for he displayed a high and confident spirit. In him the men took solace, and with his knowledge and counsel they all expected that everything would turn out to their advantage. (10)

There follows some more moving around and low-level fighting. Then, at length, the Caesarians arrive at and lay siege to the town of Thapsus (near modern Bekalta). This development forces Scipio to join battle. Our author describes the disposition of Caesar's forces, and reports:

Caesar himself quickly did the rounds of his soldiers on foot. He reminded the veterans of their bravery and their past battles, and stirred up their spirit with flattering appeals. As for the new recruits, who had never before fought in a battle, he urged them to imitate the bravery of the veterans and to eagerly seek to obtain the same fame, status and reputation by gaining victory. (81)

The battle takes place on 6 April 46 BC. The author is rather careless in describing it, given that it is the high point of his work. He does let us know, however, that Caesar's men attack precipitately, in spite of his attempts to hold them back. He also tells us that Scipio's elephants panic and stampede over their own men.

The Caesarians win. In the flush of victory, the troops slaughter their opponents, taking no prisoners. They even attack some of Caesar's own officers by mistake. We know that Caesar prided himself on his mercy (*clementia*) towards defeated enemies, and this kind of massacre was contrary to his usual policy. This naturally poses something of a problem for the author – although he seems to have no problem with uncritically reporting atrocity stories about the Pompeians. He is at pains to explain that the troops were acting against Caesar's orders. It is impossible to say how far this was true. We can, however, be fairly sure that his figures of 10,000 enemy dead to 50 Caesarians dead are incorrect.

Victory at Thapsus spells the end of the African war. The highly respected Pompeian politician Cato – a descendant of the old moralist Cato the Elder – commits suicide, in true Stoic fashion. The author tells us that he stabbed himself and then, when his doctor broke into his bedroom and tried to treat the wound, insisted on bleeding to death. Scipio is killed when his boat is sunk by Caesar's men. Caesar himself imposes fines on various individuals and cities, and then returns to Rome. He will shortly afterwards defeat the last of the Pompeians in Spain, after which he will be proclaimed *dictator perpetuus*, "dictator for life", a title which sounds more sinister in English than it did in Latin. And then we all know what happened next. Within two years of his victory at Thapsus, Caesar lay dead, and another phase in Rome's civil wars was under way.

The Pompeians' African ally King Juba didn't end up well either. He fled to Zama (modern Siliana), where the following curious encounter took place at the city gates:

> Juba spent a long time before the gates, first of all making repeated threats to the citizens of Zama, in accordance with his position of authority. Then, when he realised that he was making little progress, he begged and entreated them to let him in so that he could go to his home and his household gods. When he perceived that they were persisting in their determination, and were unmoved both by his threats and by his entreaties to let him in, he finally begged them to hand over his wives and children so that he could take them away. (91)

But the townsmen denied him even that.

The interesting thing about this scene is that the author of the book could not possibly have been present at it. We are told that the men of Zama sent envoys to Caesar, and he might have learnt about it that way; but we don't know precisely how the information reached him, nor how distorted it had become by the time it found its way into his manuscript. Other scenes in the book can be questioned in the same way. It is anyone's guess how the author knew, for example, that Cato's doctor tried to treat his wound. This highlights an important aspect of the book and its author. Livy seems at first sight to be a bit of a myth-maker, pushing the boundaries of what it means to write history; but on closer inspection he turns out to be a somewhat more conscientious and rational figure. The author of *On the African War* is an ostensibly more credible writer, but he may not be quite as credible as we might assume. Our man was undoubtedly *in* Africa, present with Caesar's army and a participant in the events which he describes. To this extent, he is an entirely different sort of historian from Livy, and potentially much more trustworthy. He was an eyewitness, for goodness' sake. Eyewitness or not, however, it is clear that he is not writing a wholly objective, factual account. We saw earlier that he is an unashamed partisan of Caesar, and we have now also seen that he can't have been an eyewitness to *everything*. He is happy to recount events which he cannot have been present at without explaining how he knew what happened.

From this perspective, it is difficult to know what to make of scenes like this:

> Labienus rode on his horse along the front line, with his head uncovered. As he did so, he urged on his own forces, and from time to time he addressed Caesar's legionaries like this: "How's it going, recruit," he said, "aren't you a brave young chap! Has that man bamboozled you too with his words? By Hercules, he's got you into a lot of trouble! I feel sorry for you." Then a soldier said, "I'm not a new recruit, Labienus, I'm a veteran of the Xth Legion." Then Labienus said, "I don't see the standards of the Xth." Then the soldier said: "Now you'll see who I am." As he spoke, he removed the helmet from his head so that the other man could see him. He drew back his javelin with all his strength and prepared to throw it at Labienus. He squarely and forcefully impaled the chest of his horse with it and said: "See, Labienus, it's a soldier of the Xth who's attacking you." (16)

This might possibly be an accurate account of a genuine encounter between the Pompeian general Labienus and a grizzled old Caesarian legionary. But it seems too good to be true – and, once again, how did the author know what happened? Was he an eyewitness? Maybe he was making up the story from whole cloth – and yet it does have a certain ring of truth about it.... Is the author perhaps describing a real encounter which passed into legionary gossip and eventually reached him through a process of Chinese whispers? We simply don't know, any more than we know what the origin of much of Livy's information was.

On the whole, however, *On the African War* is altogether closer to the street than Livy's elegantly written history. In particular, it brings home some of the more mundane realities of ancient soldiering. Where Livy might have given us heroic battle narratives, Caesar's man gives us stories of the constant attempts to secure supplies of corn, water, animal food, weapons and wood; the waiting for reinforcements; the making of work for the new recruits; the training of elephants to face battle (they were apparently equally dangerous to both sides); the cashiering of disobedient officers; the trickle of desertions from the other side; the manoeuvres and the minor skirmishes; and the Christmas 1914-style fraternisation between the two sides' soldiers. In spite of its shortcomings, a text like *On the African War* gives us just about the closest thing we are ever likely to get to a satellite broadcast direct from the ancient world.

9. The Countryside in Reality and Imagination

Most people in the ancient world lived in the countryside. So, for that matter, did most people on Earth until 2009. Classical scholars in recent years have accordingly taken a great interest in rural life. The countryside tends not to come up that often as a theme in the ancient sources themselves; but when it does appear, it can tell us some interesting things about ancient life and culture.

In our surviving texts, rural life manifests itself in quite different ways. Most ancient writers were city-dwellers, and they were either wealthy men or had wealthy patrons. They were not manure-shovelling peasants. This gave rise to a tension in classical literature. On the one hand, the countryside is a place of idyllic peace and beauty, to be admired from the safe distance of Rome or Corinth. On the other hand, we are reminded from time to time that it was a place where real people had their homes, got their hands dirty and worked for a living.

In this chapter, I want to look at two very different texts, one Greek and one Roman, which had the countryside as their theme. These will illustrate the very different ways in which ancient writers could imagine and describe rural living.

*

The first text is an 828-line poem from archaic Greece known as the *Works and Days*. It is written in the same dialect and hexameter verse as the Homeric epics, but it is a very different sort of poem. For one thing, we can be fairly sure who composed it – he was a man named Hesiod (Hésiodos). Hesiod was not a jovial, happy-go-lucky sort of person. "The earth", he declares, "is full of ills, and the sea is full of them" (101). He was one of the great pessimists of the ancient world. To put it another way, he was the first farmer to appear in Western history, and he was just as bad-tempered as all the others.

Hesiod came from a small village called Ascra in Boeotia (modern Viotia – the site has now been excavated by modern archaeologists). He depicts the place as a godforsaken hole. He calls it "miserable" and says that it is "poor in winter, hard in summer and never good" (639-640). His father was a sailor, and migrated to Ascra from a Greek-speaking settlement called Cyme in modern-day Turkey. Hesiod probably lived in or around the 600s BC. It is not clear whether he came before or after Homer, but it is generally assumed that he is the later poet. Writers in later times made up stories about the two men competing against each other; these can safely be regarded as pure fiction.

We don't know exactly how many poetic works Hesiod produced, but he is credited with composing two complete poems which survive today, the *Works and Days* and the *Theogony*. There are clear links between the two poems, and the *Theogony* was evidently composed first (the *Works and Days* refers to it, and indeed corrects it). The *Theogony*, or *Birth of the Gods*, does more or less what its title suggests. It is a kind of unfolding family tree of the pantheon of the Greek gods. It is a major source of knowledge for Greek mythology, and it bears clear signs of influence from Middle Eastern legends. One example of this is the well-known story of the succession of the chief gods. Hesiod tells us that the original chief god, Uranus, was castrated by his son Cronus (there are obvious Freudian themes here). Cronus then attempted to prevent the same thing from happening to him by the expedient of eating his children – an atrocity memorably depicted by the Spanish artist Goya. However, his son Zeus escaped, led a rebellion against him, and became the king of the gods in turn, a position which he continues to occupy today. This story has elements that must have been indigenous to the Greeks – Zeus, for example, was the Greek version of the

Indo-European sky god – but it also has definite parallels in Hittite, Mesopotamian and Levantine mythology. The Greeks learned more from those Eastern "barbarians" than they liked to admit.

Hesiod was a peasant farmer, unlike most of our other sources – but at the same time he was more than that. At the beginning of the *Theogony*, he tells a famous and mysterious story of how the Muses, the goddesses of artistic inspiration, revealed themselves to him while he was herding his sheep by Mount Helicon. This, he says, is how he was initiated into his poetic craft. As a symbol of his initiation, he reports that the goddesses gave him a staff of wood from a bay tree. He later goes on to refer again to his special relationship with the Muses in the *Works and Days*. This initiation story was much imitated in later literature, and it gave rise to an enduring link between Helicon and poetic inspiration. Quite what we should make of the story is anyone's guess. It may be a poetic fiction, but it may equally represent some kind of mystical experience which Hesiod had out in the Greek countryside, and which spurred him on to pursue a career as a poet alongside his primary vocation as a farmer.

If Hesiod is the first farmer in Western literature, he is also the first *author* – the first creator of a literary work who introduces himself to us, tells us his name and explains something to us about his life. In this, he is fundamentally different from Homer (or the bards who collectively amounted to "Homer"). The voice of the narrator in the Homeric epics is consistently impersonal and opaque, as befits someone who is claiming to present an objective narrative of events under the inspiration of the Muses. It is likely that the bardic tradition from which Homer emerged did not encourage individual singers to identify themselves, and Homer was still close enough to the tradition to maintain the convention of anonymity. Hesiod, by contrast, makes no attempt to conceal himself from us. The *Works and Days* in particular is highly personal poetry. It takes the form of advice to Hesiod's brother, Perses, who has cheated Hesiod out of his share of their inheritance by bribing the local judges in a lawsuit (or so it seems – some scholars argue that the case has not yet gone to court). The autobiographical dimension of Hesiod's poetry gives it a surprisingly modern feel. If Homer's poetic persona is anonymous and timeless, in Hesiod we have a celebrity singer who boasts about his success (he tells us that he won a major singing competition) and who makes a point of telling us the details of his family history and spiritual life.

Scholars have naturally wondered whether everything that Hesiod tells us about himself is actually *true* – did he *really* have a corrupt brother called Perses, for example, or is this a literary device? But this question is unanswerable and frankly uninteresting. It's not as if authors in *any* age can be trusted to tell the truth and only the truth about themselves in their literary works. The important point is that it is the peasant farmer Hesiod – and not, say, a king or a warrior hero – who is the first person in the Western literary record to present himself to us as an identifiable, rounded individual. When you think about it, that is pretty astonishing.

If Perses did exist, it is clear that his brother had the last laugh, because readers today are still being told by Hesiod what an arrogant wastrel he was. According to Hesiod, his only hope is to become a salt-of-the-earth small farmer like Hesiod himself. It is to him that Hesiod addresses homespun advice like the following:

> But you, Perses – always remember my command,
> and work, O son of the gods [this is obviously sarcasm],
>> so that hunger may be
> your enemy, and so that noble, fair-crowned Demeter
> may love you and may fill your storehouse with produce;
> hunger is a most fit comrade for the idle man –
> gods and men are angry at the man who lives an

idle life....

....But be pleased to set your work in order,

so that your barns are full of produce in season.

By work it is that men are many-flocked and rich;

and if they work they are much dearer to the immortals.

Work is no disgrace; idleness is a disgrace. (298-311)

This passage perhaps encapsulates the key message of the *Works and Days*. Life is tough, and Zeus has laid it down that men must work for a living. But if you get busy and work hard on your plot of land, you might just do ok.

What we have here is the closest we can ever get to the authentic voice of the archaic Greek peasant. It is poetry written by a man who has ploughed fields and planted vines with his own hands, and who has stood around the fire at the local smithy gossiping with the other farmers. Hesiod's worldview is moralistic, religious, competitive, cynical about the local lords and contemptuous of idleness. He would surely have been at home in any rural village in the ancient world (and perhaps in the modern world too). His advice certainly has a timeless rural quality to it. Honour your parents and family. Keep in with the neighbours. Don't procrastinate. Guard your tongue. Help your friends and harm your enemies. Store up food for times of hunger.

The peasant-poetry aspect of the *Works and Days* really comes into its own in the second half of the poem. This takes the form of a collection of nuggets of practical advice on agriculture and household management, much of which may be traditional or proverbial in nature. It seems to be related to the ancient Middle Eastern phenomenon of "wisdom literature", like the book of Proverbs in the Bible. This is another example of the Middle Eastern influences on Greek culture which found their way into Hesiod's poetry. Much of what Hesiod has to say in this regard is mundane, but it is oddly atmospheric too:

> Then you must fatten the curve-horned oxen in the stalls,
> for it is easy to say [to your neighbour], "Give me two oxen and a
> cart",
> but it is easy to answer, "My oxen have work to do".
> The man who thinks he is well off says that he will build a cart –
> fool, he does not know that a cart needs a hundred planks:
> take care to lay them up in your house beforehand.
> When the ploughing season first shows itself to mortal men,
> then set out, yourself and your slaves with you,
> ploughing in dry and wet weather in the ploughing season,
> hastening early, so that your fields may be filled. (452-461)

To a modern reader, this is almost a kind of email from the ancient Mediterranean countryside, in much the same way as *On the African War* comes close to being a news report from a Roman warzone. Its concerns are simple and practical – looking after livestock, ploughing the land with your slaves, the number of planks you need to build a cart. At its best, Hesiod's advice captures the scent and spirit of archaic rural life in a way that no other author does:

> And on both your feet bind boots of slaughtered ox-hide,
> tight-fitting, with their insides lined thickly with felt.
> When the frost comes in season, stitch together the
> skins of newborn kids with ox-sinew, so you may
> put them over your back to avoid the rain; on your
> head put a felt cap so your ears do not get wet;
> for cold is the dawn when Boreas [the north wind] falls still
> and at dawn there is spread over the earth a mist from
> starry heaven, over the gods' grain-bearing gifts.... (541-549)

Yet it would be a serious mistake to think that Hesiod is only concerned with the details of peasant agriculture. He locates his life as a small farmer within a much broader – indeed, cosmic – narrative of time, the gods and the human condition. A key part of this is the famous myth of the ages, according to which mankind has fallen into its current degenerate state from a Golden Age, via several intermediate stages consisting of a Silver Age, a Bronze Age and the Heroic Age of Homer's heroes. The current age is the Iron Age (the terms "Bronze Age" and "Iron Age" as used by Hesiod should not be confused with the same terms used by archaeologists). Hesiod assures us that things are going to get even worse, and that eventually Zeus will destroy us.

Hesiod has other myths too to shed light on the human condition. He tells the famous story of how Prometheus gave the gift of fire to mankind and angered Zeus in the process. Zeus redressed the balance by sending "Pandora" to the human world, a female personage created by the gods who carried a jar filled with various evils. When the evils were released, only "Elpis" remained in the jar. "Elpis" is often translated as "Hope", the point supposedly being that only Hope makes life bearable for mortals. But this makes no sense. Not only is Hesiod an unlikely person to be proclaiming the power of hope, the whole point of the story is that humans *don't* have Elpis, because it stayed behind in the jar. The word should probably be translated as "Anticipation". The point is that humans are in the dark, unable to foresee what is going to happen.

The choice of Pandora, a female, as a symbolic bearer of evil is no accident. Hesiod is a notorious misogynist. Although at times he does concede that not all women are bad, his view of the female sex is just as jaundiced as his view of other aspects of life. He has already mentioned Pandora in this context in the *Theogony*:

> For from her comes the race of females, of women,
> from her is the deadly race and tribe of women –
> a great woe for mortals – who live together with men,
> not sharing wretched poverty, but only luxury.
> (*Theogony*, 590-593)

Hesiod was preoccupied with the idea that women were greedy and represented a drain on men's resources. Reading some of his stuff is vaguely like being buttonholed in a pub by a man who insists on complaining about his alimony payments. Take these lines from the *Works and Days*:

> Do not let a tight-skirted woman deceive your mind,
> wily and chattering, trying to get your barn.
> Whoever trusts a woman – that man trusts villains.
> (373-375)

How can a man avoid the problems that women bring with them? Hesiod has some advice for managing the risk by choosing a wife carefully. Note that he is a believer in the typical ancient practice of marrying a much younger girl:

> And take a wife home for yourself at the right time,
>
> when you are not very far short of thirty years
>
> and not much over; that is the right time to marry;
>
> she should have four years of youth and marry in the fifth [i.e.
>
> > the fifth year from puberty].
>
> Marry a virgin, to teach her careful habits.
>
> Above all, marry a woman who lives nearby,
>
> looking all around you, so the neighbours do not mock you.
>
> For a man obtains nothing better than a wife
>
> who is good, but nothing grimmer than a bad one,
>
> a parasite, who burns her husband without fire,
>
> strong though he is, and sends him to a raw old age. (695-705)

History does not record Mrs Hesiod's side of the story.

*

Hesiod was the first of several ancient writers who dispensed more or less practical and realistic advice about farming and the rural world. Other such writers included Xenophon (whose thoughts about marrying teenage girls we quoted in Chapter 4), and our Roman friend Cato the Elder. Cato's *De Re Rustica (On Country Life)* is filled with just the sort of advice that one would expect from the old boy. It is typically sober and austere, and addresses such topics as animal husbandry, planting crops, draining, ploughing and manure. It deals with everything from how to cure ham to how to manage slaves. It was apparently still read with profit by farmers into the 20th century.

As we have noted, however, there were other, urban-based writers who depicted the countryside in a more idealised form. For them, it represented a beautiful and peaceful alternative to city life, offering charm, simplicity and ease. The grass was literally greener there. This mode of thinking spawned an entire genre of literature, which is known as "pastoral" or "bucolic". The pastoral tradition seems to have begun in the 3rd century BC, and was pioneered by a poet called Theocritus (born c.300 BC). Theocritus came from the Greek-speaking colonies of Sicily, but he lived and wrote in the multicultural metropolis of Alexandria. This was simultaneously a hub of commerce, culture and intellectualism – a cross between Oxbridge and New York. It was an ideal place for an immigrant Sicilian to compose pleasing fantasies about rural life, and his contemporaries duly lapped them up. Other Greek-speaking pastoral poets went on to follow in his footsteps, notably two characters called Bion and Moschus.

The typical ancient pastoral poem is set in an idyllic corner of the Mediterranean countryside – the so-called *locus amoenus* or "lovely place". It is spring or early summer. The landscape is dotted with trees and haunted by bees and cicadas, while a cool stream babbles by. The scene is populated with herdsmen who play music and sing about their love affairs. On them gaze assorted livestock, and over them hangs the supernatural presence of the goat-footed god Pan and other country deities. This is the sort of thing that I mean:

> Fortunate old man, here you'll find the cooling shade,
> among familiar streams and sacred springs.
> Here, as always, on your neighbour's boundary, the hedge,
> its willow blossoms sipped by Hybla's bees,
> will often lull you into sleep with the low buzzing:
> there, under the high cliff, the woodsman sings to the breeze:
> while the loud wood-pigeons, and the doves,
> your delight, will not cease their moaning from the tall elm.
> (*Eclogues* 1.51-58; trans. A.S.Kline)

This passage is even better in the original Latin. Even if you know no Latin, I recommend reading it aloud, right now, and then preferably re-reading it again once or twice. If in doubt, pronounce it as if it was Italian:

Fortunate senex, hic inter flumina nota
et fontis sacros frigus captabis opacum;
hinc tibi, quae semper, vicino ab limite saepes
Hyblaeis apibus florem depasta salicti
saepe levi somnum suadebit inire susurro;
hinc alta sub rupe canet frondator ad auras,
nec tamen interea raucae, tua cura, palumbes
nec gemere aeria cessabit turtur ab ulmo.

This passage comes from a work known as the *Eclogues* by the Roman poet Virgil (Publius Vergilius Maro). We have met Virgil before in his guise as an epic poet: the author of Rome's national epic, the *Aeneid*. But Virgil was not always a writer of Homeric-style heroic verse. Years before he turned his hand to the *Aeneid*, he wrote two books of poetry on country matters, the *Eclogues* and the *Georgics*. Indeed, he seems to have been a pioneer in transplanting pastoral poetry into the hard and unpromising soil of Roman Italy. His work was clearly influenced by Theocritus – and he included several *hommages* to Hesiod – but he made a very important and individual contribution to the development of the genre. After Virgil, pastoral poetry was never the same again. Apart from anything else, he seems to have been the first poet to set his pastoral verse in a place called Arcadia. The real Arcadia was a region of inland rural Greece, a backwater largely untouched by the cultural splendour of Athens and the military might of Sparta. It was a remote and impoverished place, but in the hands of Virgil and other bucolic poets it became a haven of peaceful simplicity. It has never lost this association in Western literature, right up to the time of Tom Stoppard and Seamus Heaney.

The ten *Eclogues* are classic examples of pastoral poetry, written by one of history's great literary masters. When we read them, we are taken away to a stylised world of shepherds holding singing contests among the elms and tamarisks. There is tragedy, too, in the form of lovesickness and death, just as there was in the works of the earlier Greek pastoral poets. Yet even these things are packaged in bucolic language, in a way that manages to be both witty and poignant:

Cruel Love is not sated with tears, nor grass with streams, nor bees with shrubs, nor she-goats with clover.
(10.29-30)

Even when death itself intrudes into the picture, it does so in pastoral mode, as we can see in this lament for a legendary herdsman called Daphnis:

> For Daphnis, cut off by a cruel death, the nymphs
> wept – you hazels and streams, be their witnesses –
> while his mother embraced her son's pitiful corpse
> and cried out in misery to the gods and the stars.
> In those days, no herdsmen drove their cattle,
> Daphnis, to pasture at the cool rivers, and no animal
> drank from the streams or touched the grassy fodder.
> Then, Daphnis, even the African lions cried in mourning
> for your death; so say the wild mountains and the woods.
> (5.20-28)

As I hope you can see from these extracts, Virgil paints his picture of the countryside with skill and charm. There may be a temptation to see his pastoral themes as indicating a lack of sophistication, but that would be a mistake. True, the *Eclogues* are not on the same level of depth and complexity as the *Aeneid* (although they are written in the same epic hexameter verse), but the signs of Virgil the mature poet are already apparent. In *Eclogue* 6, Virgil tells us that Apollo, the god of poetry, has expressly forbidden him from writing a martial epic. The very context in which he makes this claim, however, warns us that we don't need to take the claim at face value. *Eclogue* 6 has a pastoral setting, but it is a decidedly sophisticated composition which displays an erudite knowledge of Greek mythology and alludes to ancient scientific theories. Elsewhere in the *Eclogues*, too, we can see self-conscious artistry. In *Eclogue* 2, there is a passage in which a character imagines presenting his beloved, a boy called Alexis, with a variety of flowers and fruits, including narcissus, dill, convolvulus, quinces and African marigolds. In real life, as Virgil would have known, this ensemble could not possibly be put together, as the plants in question would never all be in season at the same time.

In more general terms, the *Eclogues* are more than just nostalgia pieces extolling the virtues of a simpler life out in the country. There is no reason to doubt that Virgil had genuine sympathy for the rural values and virtues which he describes. But, as with all the best pastoral poetry, his depiction of country life goes beyond saccharine clichés. He takes care to intersperse his bucolic idylls with references to contemporary politics and current affairs. After all, he was writing in the middle of the deadly civil wars of the late Republic. The *Eclogues* are believed to have been written, broadly speaking, on either side of the year

40 BC, when Virgil was in his early thirties. Julius Caesar had by now been assassinated (44 BC) but Augustus Caesar had not yet risen to supreme power (31 BC). At this point, indeed, Augustus was still called by his original name "Octavian": he only took on the name "Augustus" ("Revered One") in 27 BC, after he had established himself as the undisputed leader of the Roman state.

When Virgil was writing, the Roman world was experiencing a pause in the endless fighting, but it would have seemed like no more than a temporary lull. The empire was being governed by an unstable three-man commission, or "triumvirate", of Octavian, Caesar's lieutenant Mark Antony, and a nonentity by the name of Marcus Aemilius Lepidus. No-one yet knew that Octavian would succeed within a few years in establishing a stable and peaceful post-Republican regime. On the contrary, there was every reason to be pessimistic about the future. This is the background against which Virgil decided to write about his bisexual shepherds and African marigolds.

One result of the lengthy civil wars and the temporary cessation of hostilities was that there were a lot of demobilised soldiers about. The triumvirate was faced with the problem of what to do with a large number of men, battle-hardened and trained to kill, who were starting to become dangerously impatient as time passed and they failed to receive the traditional soldier's retirement package of a piece of farmland. The solution implemented by Octavian was to assume control over swathes of farmland in Italy and redistribute it to the veterans. This in turn entailed compulsorily evicting the existing farmers, or at least turning them from owners into tenants. One of the characters in *Eclogue* 1 is a goatherd called Meliboeus, who is being evicted from his farm and will accordingly need to emigrate to make a living outside of Italy. His companion Tityrus, by contrast, has successfully gone to Rome and petitioned Octavian to be allowed to keep his land – "that man will always be a god to me", he declares (1.7). This is a reflection of real-life events: the dispossessed farmers may not have been trained soldiers, but there were enough of them to threaten civil unrest, and the authorities accordingly moderated their original plans. Tityrus' story may well reflect Virgil's own life story, but it is difficult to be sure about this. Virgil does seem to put himself into the *Eclogues*, although there is nothing like the clear authorial voice of Hesiod in the *Works and Days*. He returns to the theme of the evictions in *Eclogue* 9, in which he refers explicitly to Mantua, his own place of origin. Clues like this are all he gives us.

There is a touching, and entirely deliberate, clash in the eviction poems between the pastoral world of singing goatherds and the real world of politics and war. To put it another way,

Virgil does not patronise either his characters or his audience. His poetry may not be "realistic" in the same way as the hands-dirty peasant poetry of Hesiod – his own family back in Mantua were probably affluent landowners. But it does have a striking realism of its own. The *Eclogues* are pastoral fantasies, but they are pastoral fantasies tinged with the privations of civil war-era Rome.

There are other political echoes in the collection, too. *Eclogue* 5, which we quoted from above, describes how the deceased herdsman Daphnis became a god. The similarity with the recent deification of Julius Caesar is not difficult to discern, and we know that it was not lost on ancient readers. But the most political poem in the collection is *Eclogue* 4, which is also the most famous and the least pastoral. This remarkable little piece proclaims that a divine child is about to be born during the consulship of Virgil's patron Pollio (40 BC). This event will herald the advent of a Golden Age. The natural world will bring forth its fruits in abundance without the need for human cultivation. Wool will not need to be dyed, as sheep will change the colour of their fleeces spontaneously. The cycle of time will come full circle and will begin to run again from the beginning. Heroes will mingle with gods. There will even be a repeat of the Trojan War: "great Achilles will again be sent to Troy" (4.36).

This messianic vision contrasts sharply with that of Hesiod. For the Greek poet, the Golden Age and the Heroic Age both lay in the past, far removed from the present condition of mankind. For the Roman, they were about to return. Even here, however, Virgil bears the influence of his times: even the coming Golden Age will involve war.

Who was the child in *Eclogue* 4 supposed to be? No-one knows. Inevitably, he was identified with Jesus Christ by later Christian writers, who pointed to certain echoes of Old Testament imagery in the poem; but Virgil takes care to locate the child's birth specifically in 40 BC. Even in Virgil's time, the child's identity was obscure. At least one contemporary politician, Asinius Gallus (born in 41 BC, Consul in 8 BC), seems to have claimed that it was supposed to be him. But it seems most likely that the child was always intended to be symbolic. Virgil probably didn't have an actual baby in mind.

At the very end of the collection, Virgil assumes the persona of a simple goatherd and bids farewell to his bucolic Arcadia in a set of famous lines:

> It is enough, divine Muses, for your poet to sing these lines,
> while he sits and weaves a basket of tender hibiscus....
> Let us rise. The shadows are often dangerous for singers,

the shadows of the juniper; they harm even the crops.

Go home, my well fed goats – the Evening Star is rising – go
home. (10.70-77)

There is perhaps a tinge of gentle sadness in these lines. The night is approaching, and Virgil invites us to leave his poetic pastoral world: *"Surgamus"*, "Let us rise". The tone is clearly valedictory, but what exactly is Virgil bidding farewell to? His original audience may have interpreted it as marking an end to the poetic respite provided by the *Eclogues* from the chaos of the war-torn Republic. On the other hand, with the benefit of 2,000 years of hindsight, we know that Virgil was bidding farewell only to the fantasy landscape of Arcadia. The wars were nearly over and his poetic career was just beginning.

Made in the USA
San Bernardino, CA
29 August 2015